North Carolina Standards Test Preparation and Practice

ALGEBRA 2

Evanston, Illinois • Boston • Dallas

Copyright © 2004 by McDougal Littell, a division of Houghton Mifflin Company.
All rights reserved.

Permission is hereby granted to teachers to reprint or photocopy in classroom quantities the pages or sheets in this work that carry a McDougal Littell, a division of Houghton Mifflin Company, copyright notice. These pages are designed to be reproduced by teachers for use in their classes with accompanying McDougal Littell, a division of Houghton Mifflin Company, material, provided each copy made shows the copyright notice. Such copies may not be sold and further distribution is expressly prohibited. Except as authorized above, prior written permission must be obtained from McDougal Littell, a division of Houghton Mifflin Company, to reproduce or transmit this work or portions thereof in any other form or by any other electronic or mechanical means, including any information storage or retrieval system, unless expressly permitted by federal copyright laws. Address inquiries to Supervisor, Rights and Permissions, McDougal Littell, a division of Houghton Mifflin Company, P.O. Box 1667, Evanston, IL 60204.

ISBN-13: 978-0-618-49256-5   ISBN-10: 0-618-49256-9

789—VOM—08 07

Contents

Notes to the Student   **1**

North Carolina Objectives Correlation, Algebra 2   **3**

Pre-Course Diagnostic Test   **6**
Pre-Course Skills Practice   **11**

Chapters 1–3
Chapter Standardized Tests   **16**
Building Test-Taking Skills   **22**
Practicing Test-Taking Skills   **24**
Cumulative Practice   **25**

Chapters 4–6
Chapter Standardized Tests   **28**
Building Test-Taking Skills   **34**
Practicing Test-Taking Skills   **36**
Cumulative Practice   **37**

Chapters 7–9
Chapter Standardized Tests   **40**
Building Test-Taking Skills   **46**
Practicing Test-Taking Skills   **48**
Cumulative Practice   **49**

Chapters 10–12
Chapter Standardized Tests   **52**
Building Test-Taking Skills   **58**
Practicing Test-Taking Skills   **60**
Cumulative Practice   **61**

Chapters 13–14
Chapter Standardized Tests   **64**
Cumulative Practice   **68**

Post-Course Test   **70**

Test-Taking Tips for Students   **75**
Answer Sheets for Practice Tests   **77**

End-of-Course Practice Test A   **79**
End-of-Course Practice Test B   **91**

Notes to the Student

Objectives Correlation Presents the North Carolina objectives for Algebra 2 and lists the items related to each objective that appear in the Pre-Course Diagnostic Test, Post-Course Test, and End-of-Course Practice Tests in this book.

Pre-Course Diagnostic Test Covers the material from the upcoming textbook. It provides a baseline assessment of your knowledge of course content.

Pre-Course Skills Practice Includes practice with skills that you should have from previous courses.

Chapter Standardized Tests A and B Two parallel versions of a standardized test are available for each chapter. Items are in multiple choice, short response, and extended response formats.

Building Test-Taking Skills Presents worked-out examples of test-taking skills related to multiple choice, short response, context-based multiple choice, and extended response questions.

Practicing Test-Taking Skills Offers problems that you can use to practice the skills discussed on the preceding Building Test-Taking Skills pages.

Cumulative Practice Includes material from several consecutive chapters and can be used to maintain and strengthen skills from earlier chapters.

Post-Course Test Like the Pre-Course Diagnostic Test, this covers the entire course. It provides a summative assessment of your knowledge of course content.

Test-Taking Tips for Students A summary of how to prepare for and take standardized tests.

End-of-Course Practice Tests A and B Two parallel versions of a standardized test that covers all the North Carolina objectives for the course, presented in a format similar to the North Carolina End-of-Course Test.

North Carolina Objectives Correlation, Algebra 2

	Pre-Course Diagnostic Test Item	Post-Course Test Item	Practice Test A & B Item	Textbook Lesson
Competency Goal 1: The learner will perform operations with complex numbers, matrices, and polynomials.				
1.01 Simplify and perform operations with rational exponents and logarithms (common and natural) to solve problems.	18 24	21 25	30 19 43	7.1 7.2 8.5
1.02 Define and compute with complex numbers.	14	15	10, 31, 52	5.4
1.03 Operate with algebraic expressions (polynomial, rational, complex fractions) to solve problems.	1 17 27	1 18 19 30	40 17 27 58	1.2 6.3 6.4 6.5 6.6 9.4 9.5
1.04 Operate with matrices to model and solve problems.	10	11 12 13	26 41, 54 35	4.1 4.2 4.3
1.05 Model and solve problems using direct, inverse, combined and joint variation.	4 25	4 28	5 22, 55	2.4 9.1
Competency Goal 2: The learner will use relations and functions to solve problems.				
2.01 Use the composition and inverse of functions to model and solve problems; justify results.	2 19	2 22	 3, 48 33	1.4 7.3 7.4

2.02 Use quadratic functions and inequalities to model and solve problems; justify results.
  a) Solve using tables, graphs, and algebraic properties.
  b) Interpret the constants and coefficients in the context of the problem.
	13
	
	15
		14
		
		16
			59
			11
			
			28
			56
				5.2
				5.3
				5.5
				5.6
				5.7
				5.8

Objectives Correlation, Algebra 2 *continued*

	Pre-Course Diagnostic Test Item	Post-Course Test Item	Practice Test A & B Item	Textbook Lesson
Competency Goal 2: The learner will use relations and functions to solve problems.				
2.03 Use exponential functions to model and solve problems; justify results. a) Solve using tables, graphs, and algebraic properties. b) Interpret the constants, coefficients, and bases in the context of the problem.	21 22 23	24 26 27	49 12 29 36 16	8.1 8.2 8.3 8.6 8.7 8.8
2.04 Create and use best-fit mathematical models of linear, exponential, and quadratic functions to solve problems involving sets of data. a) Interpret the constants, coefficients, and bases in the context of the data. b) Check the model for goodness-of-fit and use the model, where appropriate, to draw conclusions or make predictions.	5	5, 6 17	20, 45 18 4	2.5 5.8 8.7
2.05 Use rational equations to model and solve problems; justify results. a) Solve using tables, graphs, and algebraic properties. b) Interpret the constants and coefficients in the context of the problem. c) Identify the asymptotes and intercepts graphically and algebraically.	26 28	29 31	13, 32 6, 47 60 24	9.2 9.3 9.4 9.6
2.06 Use cubic equations to model and solve problems. a) Solve using tables and graphs. b) Interpret constants and coefficients in the context of the problem.	16	20	14 2, 57 25	6.4 6.8 7.6

Objectives Correlation, Algebra 2 *continued*

	Pre-Course Diagnostic Test Item	Post-Course Test Item	Practice Test A & B Item	Textbook Lesson
Competency Goal 2: The learner will use relations and functions to solve problems.				
2.07 Use equations with radical expressions to model and solve problems; justify results. a) Solve using tables, graphs, and algebraic properties. b) Interpret the degree, constants, and coefficients in the context of the problem.	20 29	23 32	15 37, 53 21	7.2 7.5 7.6 10.1
2.08 Use equations and inequalities with absolute value to model and solve problems; justify results. a) Solve using tables, graphs, and algebraic properties. b) Interpret the constants and coefficients in the context of the problem.	3 6	3 7	8, 51 9, 38, 44	1.7 2.8
2.09 Use the equations of parabolas and circles to model and solve problems; justify results. a) Solve using tables, graphs, and algebraic properties. b) Interpret the constants and coefficients in the context of the problem.	12 30 31	33 34	39 1 23, 50	5.1 10.2 10.3 10.6
2.10 Use systems of two or more equations or inequalities to model and solve problems; justify results. Solve using tables, graphs, matrix operations, and algebraic properties.	7 8 9 11 32	8 9 10 35	46 34 7 42	3.1 3.2 3.3 3.4 3.6 4.3 4.5 10.7

Pre-Course Diagnostic Test

1. What is the value of the expression $x^3 - 2y^2$ for $x = -4$ and $y = -5$?

   A -114 **B** -14 **C** 14 **D** 114

2. The formula $K = \frac{1}{2}mv^2$ gives the kinetic energy K of an object in terms of its mass m and velocity v. What is the equation for m?

   A $m = \frac{1}{2}Kv^2$

   B $m = \frac{\sqrt{2K}}{v}$

   C $m = \frac{2v^2}{K}$

   D $m = \frac{2K}{v^2}$

3. What is the solution of the inequality $5 \leq |2x + 1|$?

   A $x \leq -3$ or $x \geq 3$
   B $x \leq -3$ or $x \geq 2$
   C $x \leq -2$ or $x \geq 2$
   D $x \leq -2$ or $x \geq 3$

4. Which data set shows direct variation?

   A
x	1	2	3	4	5
y	8	6	4	2	0

   B
x	1	2	3	4	5
y	0.5	1	1.5	2	2.5

   C
x	1	2	3	4	5
y	2	3	4	5	6

   D
x	1	2	3	4	5
y	60	30	20	15	12

5. Which linear equation approximates the best fit to the data?

   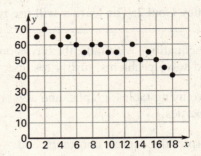

   A $y = -2x + 65$
   B $y = -5x + 100$
   C $y = -x + 68$
   D $y = -0.5x + 55$

6. What is the vertex of the graph of the absolute value function $y = -4|x + 1| + 7$?

   A $(-1, 7)$ **B** $(1, 7)$
   C $(-4, 7)$ **D** $(4, 7)$

7. What is the solution of the linear system?

   $3x - 2y = 1$
   $-x + 4y = -27$

   A $(-9, -9)$
   B $(-7, -10)$
   C $(-13, -10)$
   D $(-5, -8)$

8. At what point (x, y) does $C = 8x + 12y$ have its maximum value, subject to the following constraints?

   $0 \leq y \leq 12$
   $x + 4 \leq 16$
   $x + 2y \leq 30$

   A $(14, 6)$ **B** $(10, 12)$
   C $(12, 9)$ **D** $(18, 0)$

Pre-Course Diagnostic Test continued

9. What is the solution of the system?

   $2x - y + z = 7$
   $x + y + z = 2$
   $x - y - z = 0$

   Ⓐ $(1, 3, -2)$ Ⓑ $(1, 1, 0)$
   Ⓒ $(1, -2, 3)$ Ⓓ $(1, -1, 2)$

10. What is a simplified form of the matrix expression?

    $\begin{bmatrix} 3 & -4 \\ 1 & -1 \end{bmatrix} \begin{bmatrix} 0 & 2 \\ -5 & 3 \end{bmatrix} + \begin{bmatrix} -6 & -2 \\ 1 & 2 \end{bmatrix}$

    Ⓐ $\begin{bmatrix} 14 & -8 \\ 6 & 1 \end{bmatrix}$

    Ⓑ $\begin{bmatrix} 26 & -4 \\ 4 & -3 \end{bmatrix}$

    Ⓒ $\begin{bmatrix} -6 & -10 \\ -4 & -1 \end{bmatrix}$

    Ⓓ $\begin{bmatrix} 6 & -6 \\ -6 & -5 \end{bmatrix}$

11. The linear system below can be solved using a matrix. Which equation would you use to find the solution (x, y)?

    $-12x - 5y = 50$
    $7x + 3y = -29$

    Ⓐ $\begin{bmatrix} x \\ y \end{bmatrix} = \begin{bmatrix} -12 & -5 \\ 7 & 3 \end{bmatrix} \begin{bmatrix} 50 \\ -29 \end{bmatrix}$

    Ⓑ $\begin{bmatrix} x \\ y \end{bmatrix} = \begin{bmatrix} -3 & -5 \\ 7 & 12 \end{bmatrix} \begin{bmatrix} 50 \\ -29 \end{bmatrix}$

    Ⓒ $\begin{bmatrix} x \\ y \end{bmatrix} = \begin{bmatrix} 50 \\ -29 \end{bmatrix} \begin{bmatrix} 3 & 5 \\ -7 & -12 \end{bmatrix}$

    Ⓓ $\begin{bmatrix} x \\ y \end{bmatrix} = \begin{bmatrix} 50 \\ -29 \end{bmatrix} \begin{bmatrix} -12 & 5 \\ -7 & 3 \end{bmatrix}$

12. What is the axis of symmetry of a parabola with the equation $y = x^2 + 2x - 15$?

    Ⓐ $x = -1$ Ⓑ $x = 1$
    Ⓒ $y = -17$ Ⓓ $y = 17$

13. What is the solution of $\frac{1}{8}(x - 3)^2 = 5$?

    Ⓐ $3 + 4\sqrt{5}$ or $3 - 4\sqrt{5}$
    Ⓑ $3 + 4\sqrt{5}$ or $-3 + 4\sqrt{5}$
    Ⓒ $3 + 2\sqrt{10}$ or $3 - 2\sqrt{10}$
    Ⓓ $3 + 2\sqrt{10}$ or $-3 + 2\sqrt{10}$

14. Electrical impedance is an application of complex numbers. The impedance of a parallel circuit is found using the formula $Z = \frac{Z_1 Z_2}{Z_1 + Z_2}$, where Z_1 and Z_2 are the impedance of each pathway. What is the value of Z when $Z_1 = 2 + 3i$ and $Z_2 = 4i$?

    Ⓐ $\frac{-80 + 100i}{53}$ Ⓑ $\frac{32 + 100i}{53}$
    Ⓒ $\frac{80 - 100i}{25}$ Ⓓ $\frac{-32 - 100i}{45}$

15. What are all real and complex solutions of the equation $x^2 + 2x + 10 = 2x - 15$?

    Ⓐ -5 or 1
    Ⓑ $-2 + i\sqrt{21}$ or $-2 - i\sqrt{21}$
    Ⓒ $-5i$ or $5i$
    Ⓓ $-\sqrt{5}$ or $\sqrt{5}$

16. The volume of a prism is given by the equation $V(x) = 4x^3 + 4x^2 - 16x - 16$. What is the domain of x for which the volume V is positive?

    Ⓐ $x \geq 1$ Ⓑ $x > 1$
    Ⓒ $x \geq 2$ Ⓓ $x > 2$

Pre-Course Diagnostic Test continued

17. What is the quotient of $2x^4 + 6x^3 + 4x^2 + 7x - 15$ divided by $x + 3$?

    Ⓐ $2x^3 + 10x^2 + 7x - 5$
    Ⓑ $2x^3 + 2x^2 + 5x - 5$
    Ⓒ $2x^3 + 4x^2 - 5$
    Ⓓ $2x^3 + 4x - 5$

18. What is the simplest form of the expression? Assume all variables are positive.

    $\sqrt[3]{\dfrac{16a^4b^2}{54ab^8}}$

    Ⓐ $\dfrac{2a}{3b^2}$ Ⓑ $\dfrac{4a}{b^3}$
    Ⓒ $\dfrac{2a\sqrt[3]{2}}{b^3}$ Ⓓ $\dfrac{2a\sqrt[3]{2}}{b^2}$

19. Let $f(x) = 2x^2 + 3x$ and $g(x) = 5x - 1$. What is $g(f(x))$?

    Ⓐ $10x^2 + 15x - 1$
    Ⓑ $10x^2 + 15x - 5$
    Ⓒ $50x^2 - 5x - 1$
    Ⓓ $50x^2 - 5x - 3$

20. What is the solution of $6x^{2/3} = 24$?

    Ⓐ $2\sqrt[3]{2}$
    Ⓑ $-2\sqrt[3]{2}$ or $2\sqrt[3]{2}$
    Ⓒ -8 or 8
    Ⓓ 8

21. What is the y-intercept of the graph of the function $y = -3 \cdot 1.2^x$?

    Ⓐ -3 Ⓑ 0 Ⓒ 1.2 Ⓓ 3

22. Which is an exponential decay function?

    Ⓐ $y = 7(8.4)^x$
    Ⓑ $y = 0.24(1.03)^x$
    Ⓒ $y = 0.85(2.6)^x$
    Ⓓ $y = 4.8(0.95)^x$

23. What type of function is $f(x) = 1.02e^{1.2x}$?

    Ⓐ exponential decay function
    Ⓑ exponential growth function
    Ⓒ power function
    Ⓓ logistic growth function

24. What is $\log_3 18$ using natural logarithms?

    Ⓐ $\ln 18 - \ln 3$ Ⓑ $\ln 3 - \ln 18$
    Ⓒ $\dfrac{\ln 18}{\ln 3}$ Ⓓ $\dfrac{\ln 3}{\ln 18}$

25. The variable y varies inversely with the square of x. When $x = 4$, $y = \dfrac{1}{4}$. What is the value of y when $x = 6$?

    Ⓐ $\dfrac{1}{36}$ Ⓑ $\dfrac{1}{9}$ Ⓒ $\dfrac{1}{6}$ Ⓓ $\dfrac{2}{3}$

26. What are the domain and range of the function $y = \dfrac{x+2}{x-3} + 1$?

    Ⓐ Domain: all real numbers except -2
       Range: all real numbers except -1
    Ⓑ Domain: all real numbers except -2
       Range: all real numbers except 1
    Ⓒ Domain: all real numbers except 3
       Range: all real numbers except -1
    Ⓓ Domain: all real numbers except 3
       Range: all real numbers except 1

Pre-Course Diagnostic Test continued

27. What is the product
$$\frac{x^2 - 1}{x - 4} \cdot \frac{x + 3}{x^2 + 4x + 3}?$$
   - Ⓐ $\frac{x - 1}{x - 4}$
   - Ⓑ $\frac{x + 1}{x - 4}$
   - Ⓒ $\frac{x + 3}{x - 1}$
   - Ⓓ $\frac{x + 1}{x - 1}$

28. What is the solution of
$$\frac{x + 1}{x} = \frac{12}{x^2 - 3x}?$$
   - Ⓐ 0 or 3
   - Ⓑ −3 or 3
   - Ⓒ −3 or 5
   - Ⓓ −1 or 5

29. What is the distance between the points $(-7, 3)$ and $(-2, -9)$?
   - Ⓐ $\sqrt{61}$
   - Ⓑ 13
   - Ⓒ $\sqrt{117}$
   - Ⓓ 15

30. What is the standard form of the equation of the circle shown, whose center is the origin?

    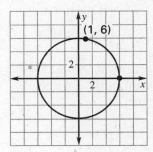

   - Ⓐ $x^2 + y^2 = 6$
   - Ⓑ $x^2 + y^2 = \sqrt{37}$
   - Ⓒ $x^2 + y^2 = 36$
   - Ⓓ $x^2 + y^2 = 37$

31. What is an equation of the parabola whose vertex is at $(2, -1)$ and whose focus is at $(2, 3)$?
   - Ⓐ $(y + 1)^2 = 4(x - 2)$
   - Ⓑ $(y + 1)^2 = -4(x - 2)$
   - Ⓒ $(x - 2)^2 = 16(y + 1)$
   - Ⓓ $(x - 2)^2 = -16(y + 1)$

32. What are the points of intersection of the graphs of the system?
$$x^2 + y^2 - 6x - 2y - 15 = 0$$
$$x^2 + y^2 - 6x + 6y + 9 = 0$$
   - Ⓐ $(3, 1)$ and $(3, -3)$
   - Ⓑ $(3, -4)$ and $(-1, -2)$
   - Ⓒ $(0, -3)$ and $(6, -3)$
   - Ⓓ $(3, 0)$ and $(0, -3)$

33. How is the series expressed with summation notation?
$$5 + 4 + 3 + 2 + 1 + 0 + (-1) + (-2)$$
   - Ⓐ $\sum_{i=1}^{8} 6 - i$
   - Ⓑ $\sum_{i=-2}^{6} i - 1$
   - Ⓒ $\sum_{i=1}^{8} 5$
   - Ⓓ $\sum_{i=2}^{5} i$

34. What is the sum of the first 20 terms of the series $3 + 5 + 7 + 9 + 11 + \cdots$?
   - Ⓐ 426
   - Ⓑ 440
   - Ⓒ 441
   - Ⓓ 462

Pre-Course Diagnostic Test continued

35. What are the first five terms of the sequence, given the first term $a_1 = 13$ and the recursive rule $a_n = a_{n-1} - n$?
    - Ⓐ 13, 12, 11, 10, 9
    - Ⓑ 13, 11, 9, 7, 5
    - Ⓒ 13, 11, 8, 4, −1
    - Ⓓ 13, 12, 10, 7, 3

36. A teacher chooses 3 students from a group of 14 to explain their project. In how many ways can she choose 3 students?
    - Ⓐ 228   Ⓑ 364   Ⓒ 1082   Ⓓ 2184

37. A number from 1 to 100 is chosen at random. What is the probability that it is divisible by 5?
    - Ⓐ $\frac{1}{100}$ Ⓑ $\frac{1}{20}$ Ⓒ $\frac{1}{10}$ Ⓓ $\frac{1}{5}$

38. The Venn diagram shows the number of people in a neighborhood of 40 people who use 3 town services: the library A, the playground B, and the jogging trail C. What is the probability that a randomly selected person from the neighborhood uses the library and playground?

    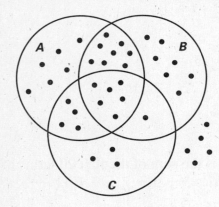

    - Ⓐ $\frac{3}{20}$ Ⓑ $\frac{1}{5}$ Ⓒ $\frac{7}{20}$ Ⓓ $\frac{4}{5}$

39. What is the arc length of a sector with radius 10 centimeters and central angle 30°?
    - Ⓐ $\frac{5\pi}{6}$ cm   Ⓑ $\frac{5\pi}{3}$ cm
    - Ⓒ 10π cm   Ⓓ 20π cm

40. What is the solution of $\sin x = -\frac{5}{6}$ where $90° \leq x \leq 270°$?
    - Ⓐ 123.6°   Ⓑ 146.4°
    - Ⓒ 213.6°   Ⓓ 236.4°

41. What is the area of a triangle with sides 8 meters, 4 meters, and 6 meters long?
    - Ⓐ 11.62 m²   Ⓑ 13.86 m²
    - Ⓒ 16.43 m²   Ⓓ 29.39 m²

42. What is the period of the function $y = \frac{3}{4} \cos \frac{\pi x}{3}$?
    - Ⓐ $\frac{3}{4}$ Ⓑ $\frac{\pi}{3}$ Ⓒ 3   Ⓓ 6

43. What is the simplified form of $\dfrac{\sin\left(\frac{\pi}{2} - x\right)}{\sin x}$?
    - Ⓐ −1   Ⓑ −tan x
    - Ⓒ cot x   Ⓓ −sec² x

44. What is a function for a sinusoid with period 4, maximum at (0, 3), and minimum at (2, 0)?
    - Ⓐ $y = 3 \cos \frac{\pi x}{2} + 1$
    - Ⓑ $y = 1.5 \cos \frac{\pi x}{2} + 1.5$
    - Ⓒ $y = -1.5 \cos \frac{\pi x}{4} + 1.5$
    - Ⓓ $y = -3 \cos \frac{\pi x}{4} + 1$

Pre-Course Skills Practice

Signed Numbers (Skills Review, pp. 905–906)

Perform the indicated operation.

1. $-8 + 7$
2. $14 - (-6)$
3. $7 \cdot 9$
4. $36 \div (-4)$
5. $13 \cdot (-3)$
6. $-12 + (-12)$
7. $-22 \div 2$
8. $-18 - 4$

Decimals, Fractions, and Percents (Skills Review, pp. 906–909)

Write as a percent.

9. 0.48
10. $\frac{23}{20}$
11. $\frac{16}{25}$
12. $\frac{13}{50}$
13. 0.03
14. 0.906
15. 0.625
16. 0.481

Write as a decimal.

17. $\frac{7}{25}$
18. 83%
19. 6%
20. 17%
21. $\frac{11}{20}$
22. 110%
23. 0.01%
24. $\frac{1}{2}\%$

Find the number.

25. 80% of 60
26. 20% of 135
27. 0.2% of 16
28. 40% of 225
29. 47% of 3
30. 130% of 17
31. 24% of 319
32. 3% of 72

Find the answer.

33. What percent of 14 is 25?
34. What percent of 62 is 50?
35. What percent of 10 is 10?
36. What percent increase is 59 to 64?
37. What percent decrease is 107 to 83?
38. What percent of 80 is 100?

Write the prime factorization of the number. If the number is prime, write *prime*.

39. 104
40. 29
41. 35
42. 83
43. 27
44. 200
45. 142
46. 54

Give the greatest common factor (GCF) and least common multiple (LCM) of the numbers.

47. 50, 14
48. 8, 15
49. 17, 34
50. 11, 12
51. 16, 44
52. 7, 9
53. 14, 49
54. 24, 60

Pre-Course Skills Practice *continued*

Proportions *(Skills Review, pp. 910–911)*

Write the ratio in two other ways.

55. $1:4$
56. 3 to 5
57. $\frac{2}{1}$
58. $\frac{2}{3}$

59. $\frac{20}{45}$
60. $1:1$
61. $4:5$
62. 3 to 10

63. 9 to 5
64. $\frac{3}{8}$
65. $5:6$
66. 4 to 3

Solve the proportion.

67. $\frac{4}{8} = \frac{x}{4}$
68. $\frac{7}{3} = \frac{14}{a}$
69. $\frac{25}{40} = \frac{c}{16}$
70. $\frac{3}{y} = \frac{21}{42}$

71. $\frac{5}{1} = \frac{20}{w}$
72. $\frac{3}{d} = \frac{18}{24}$
73. $\frac{t}{6} = \frac{1}{3}$
74. $\frac{4}{20} = \frac{10}{x}$

75. $\frac{x}{12} = \frac{120}{480}$
76. $\frac{4}{9} = \frac{c}{180}$
77. $\frac{7}{d} = \frac{21}{120}$
78. $\frac{14}{9} = \frac{70}{a}$

Significant Digits *(Skills Review, pp. 911–912)*

Perform the calculation. Write your answer with the appropriate number of significant digits.

79. $48.31 + 2.5$
80. $17 \cdot 2.333$
81. $65.28 \div 4$
82. $8000 - 21$

83. $1.004 + 2.116$
84. $5800 - 14.68$
85. $25.97 \cdot 4.32 \cdot 2.00$
86. $77.7 \div 23$

87. $15.27 + 3.142$
88. $19.409 - 13.2$
89. $6.28 \cdot 1.495$
90. $5.4 \div 1.25$

Scientific Notation *(Skills Review, p. 913)*

Write each number in scientific notation.

91. $268{,}000$
92. 0.00042
93. 0.0000058001
94. $3{,}009{,}000$

95. $61{,}000{,}000$
96. 0.000015
97. 0.00000592
98. $15{,}092{,}000{,}000$

Write each number in standard form.

99. 8.11×10^{-4}
100. 6.4×10^{7}
101. 9.80×10^{4}
102. 2.1198×10^{-3}

103. 1.04×10^{-2}
104. 4.1×10^{8}
105. 6.15×10^{-2}
106. 7.89×10^{5}

Name _____ Date _____

Pre-Course Skills Practice *continued*

Perimeter, Area, and Volume *(Skills Review, pp. 914–917)*

Find the perimeter or circumference of the figure. Then find the area.

107. a circle of radius 2 cm

108. a rectangle 3 m by 4 m

109.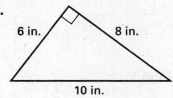

110.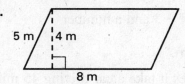

Find the surface area of the solid.

111. a cube 8 in. on a side

112. a rectangular prism 1 cm by 2 cm by 2 cm

113. a cylinder with radius 5 cm and height 8 cm

Find the volume of the solid.

114. a rectangular prism 2 cm by 3 cm by 4 cm

115. a cube 10 cm on each side

116. a cylinder with radius of 2 in. and height of 6 in.

Triangle Relationships *(Skills Review, pp. 917–918)*

Find the value of x.

117. a triangle with angles $x°$, 20°, and 80°

118. a right triangle with acute angles $x°$ and 30°

119. an isosceles triangle with vertex angle $x°$ and base angles 70°

120. an isosceles right triangle with legs 2 ft and hypotenuse x ft

121. a right triangle with hypotenuse 50 cm and legs x cm and 40 cm

Similar Figures *(Skills Review, p. 923)*

The two polygons are similar. Find the value of x.

122.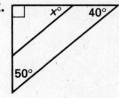

123.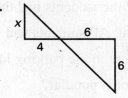

Pre-Course Skills Practice *continued*

Problem Solving *(Skills Review, pp. 929–932)*

Write the given phrase as an algebraic expression.

124. 7 times a number

125. a number minus 12

126. a number divided by 2

127. the sum of a number and 18

128. the product of -3 and a number

Solve the problem.

129. How long does it take a car driving 45 miles per hour to travel 15 miles?

130. T-shirts come in 4 sizes and 5 designs. How many T-shirt options are there?

Points in the Coordinate Plane *(Skills Review, p. 933)*

Graph the point in a coordinate plane.

131. $A(3, -4)$ **132.** $B(0, 5)$ **133.** $C(-4, -1)$ **134.** $D(-2, 0)$

Bar, Circle, and Line Graphs *(Skills Review, pp. 934–936)*

Use the graphs to answer the questions.

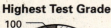
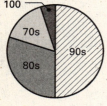
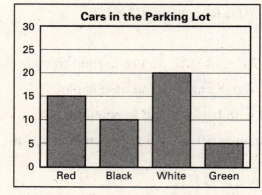

135. About what percent of the students had their highest grade in the 80s?

136. About what percent of the students had their highest grade greater than 79?

137. Complete the statement: All students had at least 1 grade above ___?___.

138. How many red cars were in the parking lot?

139. Which color car was most popular?

140. How many more white cars were in the parking lot than black cars?

141. Make a line graph to show a student's pulse rate p after m minutes of exercise.

m	5	10	15	20	25	30
p	111	116	118	125	127	127

Pre-Course Skills Practice *continued*

Opposites (Skills Review, p. 936)

Find the opposite of the number.

142. 18 **143.** −36 **144.** 15 **145.** −4

146. 73 **147.** $-\frac{1}{3}$ **148.** 9.8 **149.** −4.62

Simplify the expression.

150. $-(a - 2)$ **151.** $-(1 - x - y)$

152. $-(2x + 3y)$ **153.** $-(-a + b + c)$

154. $5x - (x - 2y)$ **155.** $m - (2p + 3m) - p$

156. $5a - (-3a + 1) - 4$ **157.** $-3d - (d + 4) - 1$

Multiplying Binomials (Skills Review, p. 937)

Simplify.

158. $(x + 3)(x - 1)$ **159.** $(3y + 1)(y - 4)$

160. $(2x + 3)(2x - 3)$ **161.** $(x + 4)(2x - 4)$

162. $(2x - 1)(x + 3)$ **163.** $(8 - x)(8 + x)$

164. $(x + 15)(x - 15)$ **165.** $(2x + 1)(2x + 1)$

Factoring (Skills Review, p. 938)

Factor.

166. $x^2 + 5x + 6$ **167.** $x^2 - 2x - 8$ **168.** $x^2 + x - 12$ **169.** $x^2 - 9x + 18$

170. $x^2 + 7x + 12$ **171.** $x^2 - 2x - 15$ **172.** $x^2 - 11x + 24$ **173.** $2x^2 + x - 3$

174. $x^2 - 49$ **175.** $x^2 + 20x + 100$ **176.** $6x^2 - 5x - 4$ **177.** $x^2 - 15x + 50$

Least Common Denominator (Skills Review, p. 939)

Find the least common denominator (LCD) of the pair of rational expressions.

178. $\frac{3}{8x}, \frac{x-1}{2x}$ **179.** $\frac{y}{4}, \frac{2}{3y}$ **180.** $\frac{1}{4mn^2}, \frac{3}{2mn}$ **181.** $\frac{1}{q^2-1}, \frac{1}{2q+2}$

182. $\frac{1-x}{x+1}, \frac{x+1}{x-1}$ **183.** $\frac{y+2}{y(y-2)}, \frac{y-2}{y+2}$ **184.** $\frac{a^2b^3}{a(a-b)}, \frac{a-b}{a^2b^2}$ **185.** $\frac{-5xyz}{x+y}, \frac{x-y}{10xy}$

Name _____   Date _____

Chapter Standardized Test 1A

Multiple Choice

1. Which list of numbers is written in increasing order?

   (A) $-\sqrt{8}, -\frac{3}{5}, -1.9, 0.8, 2$

   (B) $-1.9, -\sqrt{8}, -\frac{3}{5}, 0.8, 2$

   (C) $-\sqrt{8}, -1.9, -\frac{3}{5}, 0.8, 2$

   (D) $-1.9, -\frac{3}{5}, -\sqrt{8}, 0.8, 2$

2. Which property is illustrated by the statement $-4(7) = 7(-4)$?

   (A) Commutative property of addition
   (B) Commutative property of multiplication
   (C) Associative property of addition
   (D) Associative property of multiplication

3. What is the value of $2a^3 - b^2$ when $a = -3$ and $b = 7$?

   (A) -103 (B) -5
   (C) 5 (D) 103

4. Which number is the solution of $4y + 6 = 7(y + 3)$?

   (A) -5 (B) $-\frac{1}{3}$ (C) 1 (D) 4

5. Which number is *not* a solution of the inequality $4 + \frac{2}{3}x \leq 10$?

   (A) 0 (B) 4 (C) 9 (D) 12

6. A mural has a height h and a width 3 times its height. What is a formula for the perimeter P of the mural?

   (A) $P = 4h$ (B) $P = 4h + 3$
   (C) $P = 8h + 6$ (D) $P = 8h$

7. Which graph shows the solution to the inequality $\left|\frac{1}{2}x + 2\right| < 1$?

   (A)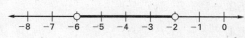

   (B)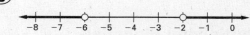

   (C)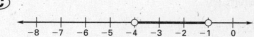

   (D)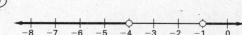

Short Response

8. Solve the formula for the area of a trapezoid for h. $A = \frac{1}{2}(b_1 + b_2)h$

Extended Response

9. Specifications for a metal rod call for the diameter to be 2.5 centimeters with an acceptable tolerance of 0.002 centimeter. Does a rod with a diameter of 2.479 centimeters meet specifications? Write an absolute value inequality that describes the acceptable diameters for the metal rods. Then solve the inequality to find the range of acceptable diameters.

Chapter Standardized Test 1B

Multiple Choice

1. Which list of numbers is written in increasing order?

   Ⓐ $2.5, 2\frac{2}{7}, 3\frac{1}{8}, \sqrt{11}, \sqrt{15}$

   Ⓑ $2\frac{2}{7}, 2.5, 3\frac{1}{8}, \sqrt{11}, \sqrt{15}$

   Ⓒ $2\frac{2}{7}, 2.5, \sqrt{11}, 3\frac{1}{8}, \sqrt{15}$

   Ⓓ $2.5, 2\frac{2}{7}, \sqrt{11}, 3\frac{1}{8}, \sqrt{15}$

2. Which property is illustrated by the statement $8 + (7 + 11) = (8 + 7) + 11$?

   Ⓐ Commutative property of addition
   Ⓑ Commutative property of multiplication
   Ⓒ Associative property of addition
   Ⓓ Associative property of multiplication

3. What is the value of $3a^3 - b^4$ when $a = -4$ and $b = 2$?

   Ⓐ -208 Ⓑ -176
   Ⓒ 176 Ⓓ 208

4. Which number is the solution of $3(b + 3) = b + 14$?

   Ⓐ $2\frac{1}{2}$ Ⓑ $5\frac{1}{2}$ Ⓒ 8 Ⓓ $11\frac{1}{2}$

5. Which number is a solution of the inequality $2x + 7 > 1$?

   Ⓐ -6 Ⓑ -4 Ⓒ -3 Ⓓ -1

6. A cylinder has a diameter 3 times its height. What is a formula for its volume V in terms of its height h?

   Ⓐ $V = \frac{3}{2}\pi h^3$ Ⓑ $V = \frac{9}{4}\pi h^3$
   Ⓒ $V = 3\pi h^3$ Ⓓ $V = 9\pi h^3$

7. Which graph shows the solution to the inequality $|x + 1| \geq 3$?

   Ⓐ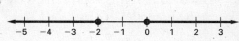

   Ⓑ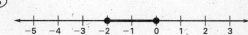

   Ⓒ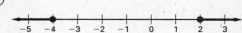

   Ⓓ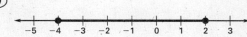

Short Response

8. Solve the equation $y = \frac{1}{3}x(z + 1)$ for z.

Extended Response

9. Specifications for an optical lens state that the ideal thickness is 6.5 millimeters. The acceptable tolerance is 0.0625 millimeters. Does a lens with a thickness of 6.475 millimeters meet specifications? Write an absolute value inequality that describes the acceptable thicknesses for a lens. Then solve the inequality to find the range of acceptable thicknesses.

Chapter Standardized Test 2A

Multiple Choice

1. If $f(x) = -x^2 - 5x + 3$, what is $f(-3)$?
   Ⓐ -21 Ⓑ -3 Ⓒ 9 Ⓓ 27

2. What is the slope of the line that passes through $(-4, 1)$ and $(2, -3)$?
   Ⓐ $-\frac{4}{3}$ Ⓑ -1 Ⓒ $-\frac{2}{3}$ Ⓓ $-\frac{1}{2}$

3. Which equation is represented by the graph shown?

   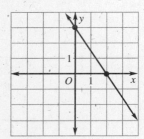

   Ⓐ $y = -\frac{3}{2}x + 3$ Ⓑ $y = \frac{3}{2}x + 3$
   Ⓒ $y = -\frac{2}{3}x + 3$ Ⓓ $y = \frac{2}{3}x + 3$

4. What is the equation of the line that passes through $(0, -1)$ and $(3, 1)$?
   Ⓐ $y = \frac{3}{2}x + 1$
   Ⓑ $y = \frac{3}{4}x - 1$
   Ⓒ $y = -\frac{3}{2}x + 1$
   Ⓓ $y = \frac{2}{3}x - 1$

5. What is the range of the function $y = 3 - |x - 1|$?
   Ⓐ $y \geq 0$ Ⓑ $y \geq 4$
   Ⓒ $y \leq 2$ Ⓓ $y \leq 3$

6. Which of the following is the closest approximation of the best-fitting line for the data in the scatter plot?

   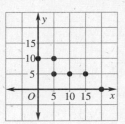

   Ⓐ $y = -\frac{1}{2}x + 15$ Ⓑ $y = -\frac{1}{2}x + 10$
   Ⓒ $y = -x + 5$ Ⓓ $y = -x + 10$

7. You have a budget of $100 to spend on books and movies. A book costs $19 and a movie costs $15. Which inequality describes the amount of books b and movies m you can buy?
   Ⓐ $15b + 19m \leq 100$
   Ⓑ $15b + 19m \geq 100$
   Ⓒ $19b + 15m \leq 100$
   Ⓓ $19b + 15m \geq 100$

8. If $f(x) = \begin{cases} 3x + 10, & \text{if } x < 10 \\ 2.5x, & \text{if } x \geq 10 \end{cases}$, what is $f(12)$?
   Ⓐ 25 Ⓑ 30 Ⓒ 40 Ⓓ 46

Short Response

9. Graph the inequality $4x - 2y < 0$ on a coordinate plane.

Extended Response

10. Graph the three functions on one coordinate plane. Explain the relationships among the graphs.
    $y = |x|$
    $y = |x| + 2$
    $y = |x| - 2$

Chapter Standardized Test 2B

Multiple Choice

1. If $f(x) = -3x^2 + 4x - 1$, what is $f(4)$?
   Ⓐ -65 Ⓑ -33 Ⓒ -21 Ⓓ 31

2. What is the slope of the line that passes through $(-3, -3)$ and $(5, 1)$?
   Ⓐ $-\frac{1}{2}$ Ⓑ -1 Ⓒ $\frac{1}{2}$ Ⓓ 2

3. Which equation is represented by the graph shown?

   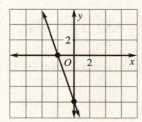

   Ⓐ $y = -\frac{1}{3}x - 3$ Ⓑ $y = -3x - 3$
   Ⓒ $y = -\frac{1}{3}x - 6$ Ⓓ $y = -3x - 6$

4. What is the equation of the line that passes through $(0, 4)$ and $(3, 2)$?
   Ⓐ $y = -\frac{3}{2}x + 4$
   Ⓑ $y = -\frac{3}{2}x + 2$
   Ⓒ $y = -\frac{2}{3}x + 4$
   Ⓓ $y = -\frac{2}{3}x + 2$

5. What is the range of the function $y = |4 - 2x|$?
   Ⓐ $y \geq 0$ Ⓑ $y \geq 2$
   Ⓒ $y \leq 2$ Ⓓ $y \leq 4$

6. Which of the following is the closest approximation of the best-fitting line for the data in the scatter plot?

   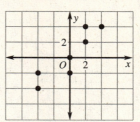

   Ⓐ $y = 2x$ Ⓑ $y = x$
   Ⓒ $y = 3x - 2$ Ⓓ $y = x - 2$

7. You have 3.5 hours to work on English and history. You can write 1.2 pages of your history assignment each hour and 1.75 pages of your English assignment each hour. Which inequality describes the pages of history h and English e you can write?
   Ⓐ $1.2h + 1.75e \geq 3.5$
   Ⓑ $1.2h + 1.75e \leq 3.5$
   Ⓒ $1.75h + 1.2e \geq 3.5$
   Ⓓ $1.75h + 1.2e \leq 3.5$

8. If $f(x) = \begin{cases} 45 - 2x, & \text{if } x < 22 \\ 45 - x, & \text{if } x \geq 22 \end{cases}$, what is $f(20)$?
   Ⓐ 1 Ⓑ 5 Ⓒ 11 Ⓓ 13

Short Response

9. Graph the inequality $3x + 2y \geq 2$ on a coordinate plane.

Extended Response

10. Graph the three functions on one coordinate plane. Explain the relationships among the graphs.
    $y = |x|$ $y = |x - 2|$
    $y = |x + 2|$

Chapter Standardized Test 3A

Multiple Choice

1. Which linear system has no solution?
   - **A** $-x + 2y = 7$
     $-2x + 2y = 7$
   - **B** $3x + 2y = 0$
     $6x + 4y = 2$
   - **C** $x - y = 2$
     $-x + y = -2$
   - **D** $5x + y = -3$
     $4x + 2y = 7$

2. Which ordered pair is a solution of the linear system?
   $-2x + y = -8$
   $3x - 2y = 13$
   - **A** $(3, -2)$
   - **B** $(-4, -16)$
   - **C** $(1, -6)$
   - **D** $(-1, -10)$

3. Which linear system is graphed below?

   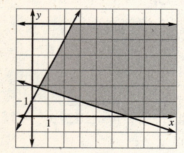

   - **A** $y \leq 6$
     $y \leq 2x + 1$
     $y \geq -\frac{1}{3}x + 2$
   - **B** $y \leq 7$
     $y \geq 2x + 1$
     $y \geq -\frac{1}{3}x + 2$
   - **C** $y \geq 0$
     $y \leq 6$
     $y \geq -\frac{1}{3}x + 2$
     $y \leq 2x + 1$
   - **D** $y \geq 0$
     $y \leq 6$
     $y \geq 2x + 1$
     $y \leq -\frac{1}{3}x + 2$

4. What is the minimum value of the objective function $C = 3x - y$, subject to the following constraints?
   $0 \leq x \leq 20$
   $y \geq 5$
   $-x + 2y \leq 20$
   - **A** -10
   - **B** -5
   - **C** 40
   - **D** 55

5. What is the value of z in the linear equation when $x = 2$ and $y = -2$?
   $8x - 2y + 5z = 10$
   - **A** $-2\frac{1}{5}$
   - **B** -2
   - **C** $-\frac{2}{5}$
   - **D** $\frac{2}{5}$

6. Which ordered triple is a solution of the linear system?
   $x + 2y - z = -9$
   $x - y + z = 8$
   $2x + y + z = 3$
   - **A** $(0, -1, 7)$
   - **B** $(-1, 1, 10)$
   - **C** $(-2, 3, 13)$
   - **D** $(1, -3, 4)$

Short Response

7. Violet Lang is starting a small business selling homemade jams. She invests $450 in equipment and marketing. Each jar of jam costs her $1.20 to make, and she sells them for $3. How many jars must she sell to break even? Show your work.

Extended Response

8. Your class is selling T-shirts as a fundraiser. You can buy and print a child's T-shirt for $6 and sell it for $8. You can buy and print an adult's T-shirt for $7 and sell it for $10. You can spend $280 to buy and print the T-shirts, and you estimate you can sell, at most, 20 children's shirts. Find the number of shirts you should buy to maximize your profit. Explain your reasoning.

Chapter Standardized Test 3B

Multiple Choice

1. Which linear system has no solution?

   A $-3x + y = 5$
   $4x + 2y = 5$

   B $4x - 2y = -6$
   $2x - y = -3$

   C $4x - 3y = 2$
   $8x - 6y = 3$

   D $x + 2y = -1$
   $3x + 4y = 6$

2. Which ordered pair is a solution of the linear system?

   $4x - 2y = -2$
   $2x + y = 9$

   A $(2, 5)$ **B** $(0, 1)$
   C $(3, 3)$ **D** $(-1, 11)$

3. Which linear system is graphed below?

   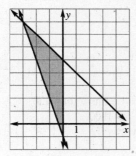

   A $x \geq 0$
   $y \leq -x + 5$
   $y \geq -3x - 1$

   B $x \geq 0$
   $y \leq -3x - 1$
   $y \geq -x + 5$

   C $x \leq 0$
   $y \leq -x + 5$
   $y \geq -3x - 1$

   D $x \leq 0$
   $y \leq -3x - 1$
   $y \geq -x + 5$

4. What is the maximum value of the objective function $P = 2x + y$, subject to the following constraints?

   $0 \leq x \leq 10$
   $y \geq 4$
   $x + 2y \leq 24$

   A 15 **B** 24 **C** 27 **D** 32

5. What is the value of x in the linear equation when $y = 3$ and $z = -1$?

   $-2x + y + 4z = 9$

   A -8 **B** -5 **C** -1 **D** $\frac{1}{2}$

6. Which ordered triple is a solution of the linear system?

   $2x + 2y - z = -9$
   $x + y + z = 3$
   $x - y + 2z = 8$

   A $(2, -1, 4)$ **B** $(4, 2, 3)$
   C $(-4, 7, 3)$ **D** $(-2, 0, 5)$

Short Response

7. Tom Wang is starting a small business selling specialty fishing flies. He invests $390 in equipment and marketing. Each fly costs him $2.50 to make, and he sells them for $4.50. How many flies must he sell to break even? Show your work.

Extended Response

8. Your club is selling babysitting services one Saturday night as a fundraiser. You charge $15 for children picked up by 9 P.M., and $30 for kids who are picked up by midnight. You can handle, at most, 30 children. You expect at least 6 children to be picked up at the earlier time, and you cannot have more than 20 who want to stay late. Find the number of early and late pick-ups you should have to maximize your profit. Explain your reasoning.

Name _____ Date _____

Building Test-Taking Skills
For use after Chapters 1–3

Strategies for Answering
Multiple Choice Questions

The strategies below can help you answer a multiple choice question. You can also use these strategies to check whether your answer to a multiple choice question is reasonable.

Strategy: Estimate the Answer

Problem 1

You will use powers and exponents to solve this problem.

The table shows how many pennies you save each day. If the pattern continues, what is the first day you will save more than ten dollars worth of pennies?

Day	1	2	3
Pennies	$2^1 = 2$	$2^2 = 4$	$2^3 = 8$

A. Day 8
B. Day 9
C. Day 10
D. Day 11

Estimate: 2^8 is a little more than 250, so $2^9 > 500$ and $2^{10} > 1000$. The correct answer is C.

Strategy: Use Visual Clues

Problem 2

The garden's area is 900 square feet. Use the Guess, Check, and Revise strategy to find the length of one side of the garden. Each side of the garden is 30 feet long.

How many feet of fencing do you need to enclose the square garden shown?

A. 30 ft
B. 60 ft
C. 90 ft
D. 120 ft

900 ft²

Multiply the side length by 4 to find the total amount of fencing needed. To enclose the garden, you need 120 feet of fencing. The correct answer is D.

Algebra 2
North Carolina Standards Test Preparation and Practice

Copyright © McDougal Littell,
a division of Houghton Mifflin Company.

Name _____   Date _____

Building Test-Taking Skills *continued*
For use after Chapters 1–3

Strategy: Use Number Sense

Problem 3

The problem involves integers, not fractions or decimals.

When multiplying a positive integer by a negative integer, the product is __?__ .

A. greater than the positive integer

B. greater than the negative integer

C. less than or equal to the negative integer

D. less than the negative integer

The sign is negative and the absolute value of the product is greater than or equal to either factor. C is the correct answer.

Eliminating Unreasonable Choices The strategies used to find the correct answers for Problems 1–3 are the same strategies you can use to eliminate answer choices that are unreasonable or obviously incorrect.

Problem 4

Read the problem carefully. Degrees Fahrenheit are 32° more than almost twice the temperature in degrees Celsius.

The average body temperature of a polar bear is 37°C. Use the formula $F = 1.8C + 32$ to find the temperature in degrees Fahrenheit.

A. 34°F ············· *Not* correct. A temperature of about 1°C is 34°F.

B. 69°F

C. 74.95°F

D. 98.6°F ············· $1.8(37) + 32 = 98.6$, so the correct answer is D.

Watch Out! Some answers that appear correct at first glance may be incorrect. Be aware of common errors.

Your turn now

Explain why the selected answer choice is unreasonable.

1. Two times a number plus 7 is -21. What is the number?

   A. -14 B. -7 ✗ C. 7   D. 14

2. Your school earns $1.50 for every T-shirt sold. Find the minimum number of T-shirts you must sell in order to raise $500.

   A. 333   B. 334   C. 500   ✗ D. 750

Algebra 2   23
North Carolina Standards Test Preparation and Practice

Name _____   Date _____

Practicing Test-Taking Skills
For use after Chapters 1–3

Multiple Choice

1. Which graph represents $|-3x - 4| \geq 2$?

   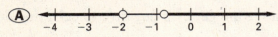

2. Which ordered triple, (a, b, c), is the solution of the system?

   $a + 2b + 5c = -1$
   $2a - b + c = 2$
   $3a + 4b - 4c = 14$

   (A) $(2, 1, 1)$ (B) $(2, 1, -1)$
   (C) $(0, 1, 1)$ (D) $(-2, 1, 1)$

3. Which line best fits the scatter plot?

   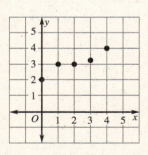

   (A) $y = x + 2$ (B) $y = x$
   (C) $y = \frac{1}{2}x + 2$ (D) $y = 3$

4. Miguel has n nickels and d dimes. He has at most 12 coins, and the value of the money is no more than $2.00. Which system represents this situation?

   (A) $n + d \leq 12$ (B) $n + d = 12$
       $5n + 10d \leq 200$ $5n + 10d = 200$
   (C) $n + d \leq 12$ (D) $n + d < 12$
       $10n + 5d \leq 200$ $5n + 10d < 200$

5. The variable t varies directly with x. The constant of variation is a. Which of the following is false?

   (A) $t = xa$ (B) $x = \dfrac{t}{a}$
   (C) $a = \dfrac{t}{x}$ (D) $a = \dfrac{x}{t}$

6. Which system of linear equations is represented by the diagram below?

   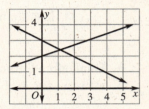

   (A) $-x + 3y = 6$ (B) $-3x + y = 6$
       $x + 2y = 6$ $2x + y = 6$
   (C) $-x + y = 6$ (D) $-2x + y = 6$
       $2x + y = 6$ $3x + y = 6$

7. Which function represents this table of data?

x	0	1	2	5
$f(x)$	4	7	10	19

   (A) $f(x) = 2x + 4$ (B) $f(x) = 3x + 4$
   (C) $f(x) = 2x - 3$ (D) $f(x) = 3x - 4$

8. The ideal weight of a full can of tomatoes is 16 ounces. Let t represent the actual weight of a can of tomatoes. If t differs from the ideal weight by more than 0.25 ounces, the can will be rejected. Which inequality represents acceptable weights?

   (A) $16 - t \leq 0.25$ (B) $|16 - t| \leq 0.25$
   (C) $|16 - t| \geq 0.25$ (D) $16 - t \geq 0.25$

Cumulative Practice

For use after Chapters 1–3

Chapter 1

Multiple Choice In Exercises 1–7, choose the letter of the correct answer.

1. Which statement is true? *(Lesson 1.1)*

    Ⓐ $\sqrt{3} \geq 3$

    Ⓑ $\frac{3}{8} \geq \frac{4}{9}$

    Ⓒ $1.336 \geq 1.363$

    Ⓓ $1\frac{3}{5} \geq 1.6$

2. What is a simplified form of $4x + y - 3 + 2y - 3x - 1$? *(Lesson 1.2)*

    Ⓐ $x + 3y - 4$

    Ⓑ $4x + 3y - 1$

    Ⓒ $6x - 2y - 4$

    Ⓓ $4x - 4$

3. A consultant's base fee is $2000 for an evaluation, plus 10% of any cost savings over the next year. Which equation could represent the total paid to the consultant? *(Lesson 1.3)*

    Ⓐ $y = 2000x$

    Ⓑ $y = 10x + 2000$

    Ⓒ $y = 0.1x + 2000$

    Ⓓ $y = 2000x + 10$

4. The force on a current-carrying wire in a magnetic field is $F = BIL$, where F is the force, B is the strength of the magnetic field, I is the current, and L is the length of the wire in the field. What is an equation for current? *(Lesson 1.4)*

    Ⓐ $I = \frac{F}{BL}$ Ⓑ $I = \frac{BL}{F}$

    Ⓒ $I = FBL$ Ⓓ $I = \frac{FL}{B}$

5. What are the next 3 numbers in the pattern? *(Lesson 1.5)*

    95, 91, 87, 83, 79, . . .

    Ⓐ 76, 72, 68   Ⓑ 75, 71, 67

    Ⓒ 76, 71, 66   Ⓓ 75, 72, 69

6. What is the solution of $3 \leq 2x + 7 \leq 21$? *(Lesson 1.6)*

    Ⓐ $5 \leq x \leq 14$ Ⓑ $3 \leq 2x \leq 21$

    Ⓒ $-2 \leq x \leq 7$ Ⓓ $5 \leq x < 7$

7. What is the solution of $|-3x + 5| > 7$? *(Lesson 1.7)*

    Ⓐ $x < -\frac{2}{3}$ or $x > 4$

    Ⓑ $x < \frac{2}{3}$ or $x > 4$

    Ⓒ $-\frac{2}{3} < x < 4$

    Ⓓ $-4 < x < \frac{2}{3}$

8. **Short Response** Write an expression for the perimeter of an equilateral triangle with sides of length $2x + y$. Evaluate the expression for $x = 8$ and $y = 11$. *(Lesson 1.2)*

9. **Extended Response** An internet café charges $.25 per minute for online access. You must purchase at least 5 minutes and cannot be online for more than 60 minutes. *(Lesson 1.6)*

    a. Write a compound inequality for the time you can be online.

    b. Write a compound inequality for the charge.

    c. What is the charge for 32 minutes online?

Cumulative Practice continued

For use after Chapters 1–3

Chapter 2

Multiple Choice In Exercises 10–15, choose the letter of the correct answer.

10. What is the value of the equation $f(x) = -8x + 4$ when $x = 3$? *(Lesson 2.1)*
    - Ⓐ -24
    - Ⓑ -20
    - Ⓒ -12
    - Ⓓ 28

11. Which pair of lines are perpendicular? *(Lesson 2.2)*
    - Ⓐ Line 1: through $(4, 6)$ and $(5, -1)$
      Line 2: through $(-2, 4)$ and $(3, -3)$
    - Ⓑ Line 1: through $(1, 4)$ and $(4, -2)$
      Line 2: through $(-1, 3)$ and $(0, 5)$
    - Ⓒ Line 1: through $(2, 8)$ and $(4, 2)$
      Line 2: through $(-2, 0)$ and $(1, 1)$
    - Ⓓ Line 1: through $(-5, -3)$ and $(0, 4)$
      Line 2: through $(-4, 1)$ and $(1, 8)$

12. What is the y-intercept of the graph of $5x + 3y = -1$? *(Lesson 2.3)*
    - Ⓐ $-\frac{5}{3}$
    - Ⓑ -1
    - Ⓒ $-\frac{1}{3}$
    - Ⓓ $\frac{5}{3}$

13. Which equation represents the line with slope $\frac{4}{5}$ that passes through $(10, 29)$? *(Lesson 2.4)*
    - Ⓐ $y = \frac{4}{5}x + 37$
    - Ⓑ $y = \frac{4}{5}x - 37$
    - Ⓒ $y = \frac{4}{5}x + 21$
    - Ⓓ $y = \frac{4}{5}x - 21$

14. Which of the following is true of the relationship between the high temperature and the number of hours of daylight in a day in North Carolina? *(Lesson 2.5)*
    - Ⓐ positive correlation
    - Ⓑ negative correlation
    - Ⓒ no correlation
    - Ⓓ not enough information

15. Which ordered pair is a solution of the inequality $-3x + 5y > 8$? *(Lesson 2.6)*
    - Ⓐ $(0, 0)$
    - Ⓑ $(-1, 1)$
    - Ⓒ $(1, -1)$
    - Ⓓ $(1, 3)$

16. **Short Response** What are the coordinates of the vertex of the graph of $y = 3|x + 4| - 7$? *(Lesson 2.8)*

17. **Extended Response** A residential snow-plowing business charges $200 minimum per season, plus an additional $15 for each plowing after the first 10. *(Lesson 2.7)*

    a. Write a piecewise function to represent the total cost of plowing a residence over the season.

    b. Evaluate the function for 5, 12, and 20 plowings.

Cumulative Practice continued

For use after Chapters 1–3

Chapter 3

Multiple Choice In Exercises 18–23, choose the letter of the correct answer.

18. Which of the following ordered pairs is a solution of the linear system below?
    (Lessons 3.1, 3.2)

    $4x - y = 8$
    $2x + 3y = 18$

    Ⓐ (2, 0)   Ⓑ (1, −4)
    Ⓒ (3, 4)   Ⓓ (6, 2)

19. Which linear system has *infinitely many* solutions? *(Lesson 3.2)*

    Ⓐ $-x + 3y = 2$
       $2x - y = 6$

    Ⓑ $4x + 2y = 7$
       $2x + y = -3$

    Ⓒ $-2x + 6y = 8$
       $-3x + 8y = 10$

    Ⓓ $3x - 6y = 9$
       $-x + 2y = -3$

20. Which inequality is *not* shown in the system graphed below? *(Lesson 3.3)*

    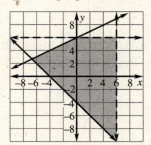

    Ⓐ $y \geq \frac{1}{2}x + 6$ Ⓑ $y < 6$
    Ⓒ $y \geq -x - 4$ Ⓓ $x < 6$

21. Joe can paint 2.5 walls per hour, and Ray can paint 2 walls per hour. They want to paint an apartment with 16 walls. Ray can paint at most 4 hours. Which of the following correctly shows the constraints for the time j Joe paints and the time r Ray paints? *(Lesson 3.4)*

    Ⓐ $j \geq 0$
       $0 \leq r \leq 4$
       $2j + 2.5r \leq 16$

    Ⓑ $j \geq 0$
       $0 \leq r \leq 4$
       $2.5j + 2r \leq 16$

    Ⓒ $0 \leq r \leq 4$
       $2j + 2.5r \leq 16$

    Ⓓ $0 \leq r \leq 4$
       $2.5j + 2r \leq 16$

22. Which point is located in the *xz*-plane of a three-dimensional coordinate system?
    (Lesson 3.5)

    Ⓐ (4, 0, −8)   Ⓑ (0, 6, 0)
    Ⓒ (2, 0, −6)   Ⓓ (−1, −1, −1)

23. What is the solution, if any, of the system below? *(Lesson 3.6)*

    $x + 2y - z = 2$
    $-x + y + z = 1$
    $-x - 2y + z = 0$

    Ⓐ (2, 1, 2)   Ⓑ (−1, 1, 0)
    Ⓒ no solution   Ⓓ many solutions

24. **Short Response** Plot the ordered triple (1, 3, 0) on a three-dimensional coordinate system. *(Lesson 3.5)*

25. **Extended Response** Given the following constraints, find the minimum and maximum values of the objective function $C = 50x + 28y$. *(Lesson 3.4)*

    Constraints: $y \leq 16$
    $y \leq x + 8$
    $y \geq -x + 8$

Chapter Standardized Test 4A

Multiple Choice

1. Which matrix equals
$3\begin{bmatrix} 1 & 8 \\ -4 & -3 \end{bmatrix} - 2\begin{bmatrix} 5 & 2 \\ 0 & -1 \end{bmatrix}?$

   Ⓐ $\begin{bmatrix} 13 & 28 \\ -12 & -11 \end{bmatrix}$ Ⓑ $\begin{bmatrix} -2 & 22 \\ -12 & -8 \end{bmatrix}$

   Ⓒ $\begin{bmatrix} 3 & 24 \\ -12 & -9 \end{bmatrix}$ Ⓓ $\begin{bmatrix} -7 & 20 \\ -12 & -7 \end{bmatrix}$

2. What is the product of
$\begin{bmatrix} 8 & 1 & -2 \\ 3 & 4 & 0 \\ -1 & 6 & 2 \end{bmatrix}$ and $\begin{bmatrix} -1 & 0 & 4 \\ 0 & -3 & -2 \\ 1 & 2 & 1 \end{bmatrix}?$

   Ⓐ $\begin{bmatrix} -8 & -3 & 9 \\ 2 & -4 & 0 \\ 7 & -6 & 4 \end{bmatrix}$

   Ⓑ $\begin{bmatrix} -10 & -7 & 28 \\ -3 & -12 & 4 \\ 3 & -14 & -14 \end{bmatrix}$

   Ⓒ $\begin{bmatrix} 5 & 31 & -13 \\ -1 & 20 & -6 \\ 3 & 5 & 19 \end{bmatrix}$

   Ⓓ $\begin{bmatrix} -7 & -6 & 11 \\ -4 & -10 & 16 \\ -8 & -13 & 4 \end{bmatrix}$

3. What is the determinant of $\begin{bmatrix} 5 & -6 \\ -3 & 4 \end{bmatrix}?$

   Ⓐ 2 Ⓑ 8
   Ⓒ 14 Ⓓ 38

4. What is the inverse of $\begin{bmatrix} 3 & 1 \\ -2 & 1 \end{bmatrix}?$

   Ⓐ $\begin{bmatrix} \frac{1}{3} & -\frac{1}{3} \\ \frac{2}{3} & 1 \end{bmatrix}$ Ⓑ $\begin{bmatrix} \frac{1}{5} & -\frac{1}{5} \\ \frac{2}{5} & \frac{3}{5} \end{bmatrix}$

   Ⓒ $\begin{bmatrix} \frac{1}{3} & -\frac{2}{3} \\ \frac{1}{3} & 1 \end{bmatrix}$ Ⓓ $\begin{bmatrix} \frac{1}{5} & -\frac{2}{5} \\ \frac{1}{5} & \frac{3}{5} \end{bmatrix}$

5. Which system corresponds to the matrix equation shown below?

   $\begin{bmatrix} 87 & 41 \\ 13 & -56 \end{bmatrix} \begin{bmatrix} x \\ y \end{bmatrix} = \begin{bmatrix} -530 \\ -2440 \end{bmatrix}$

   Ⓐ $87x + 41y = -530$
   $13x - 56y = -2440$

   Ⓑ $87x + 13y = -530$
   $41x - 56y = -2440$

   Ⓒ $87x - 56y = -530$
   $41x + 13y = -2440$

   Ⓓ $87x + 13y = -2440$
   $41x - 56y = -530$

Short Response

6. Use an inverse matrix to find the solution of the following linear system.

   $3x + 2y = -2$
   $2x - y = 15$

Extended Response

7. What is the area of a triangle with vertices $(4, 2)$, $(-3, 6)$, and $(7, 1)$?

Chapter Standardized Test 4B

Multiple Choice

1. Which matrix equals
$2\begin{bmatrix} 5 & 0 \\ -6 & 2 \end{bmatrix} - 4\begin{bmatrix} -3 & 2 \\ -1 & -2 \end{bmatrix}?$

   Ⓐ $\begin{bmatrix} 7 & 2 \\ -13 & 2 \end{bmatrix}$ Ⓑ $\begin{bmatrix} 22 & -8 \\ -8 & 12 \end{bmatrix}$

   Ⓒ $\begin{bmatrix} 13 & -2 \\ -11 & 6 \end{bmatrix}$ Ⓓ $\begin{bmatrix} -2 & 8 \\ -16 & -4 \end{bmatrix}$

2. What is the product of
$\begin{bmatrix} 1 & -1 & -2 \\ 0 & 5 & -1 \\ 2 & 3 & 0 \end{bmatrix}$ and $\begin{bmatrix} 3 & 1 & 2 \\ 2 & -1 & 1 \\ 0 & -2 & 1 \end{bmatrix}?$

   Ⓐ $\begin{bmatrix} 1 & -4 & 8 \\ 3 & -2 & 1 \\ -9 & 4 & -3 \end{bmatrix}$

   Ⓑ $\begin{bmatrix} 14 & 1 & 22 \\ -2 & -6 & 3 \\ -3 & 10 & -7 \end{bmatrix}$

   Ⓒ $\begin{bmatrix} 3 & 9 & -8 \\ 0 & -1 & 4 \\ -5 & 17 & -9 \end{bmatrix}$

   Ⓓ $\begin{bmatrix} 1 & 6 & -1 \\ 10 & -3 & 4 \\ 12 & -1 & 7 \end{bmatrix}$

3. What is the determinant of $\begin{bmatrix} -7 & -4 \\ 3 & 5 \end{bmatrix}?$

   Ⓐ -47 Ⓑ -23
   Ⓒ 23 Ⓓ 47

4. What is the inverse of $\begin{bmatrix} 1 & -1 \\ -3 & 6 \end{bmatrix}?$

   Ⓐ $\begin{bmatrix} \frac{2}{3} & \frac{1}{9} \\ \frac{1}{3} & \frac{1}{9} \end{bmatrix}$ Ⓑ $\begin{bmatrix} 2 & \frac{1}{3} \\ \frac{1}{3} & \frac{2}{3} \end{bmatrix}$

   Ⓒ $\begin{bmatrix} 2 & \frac{1}{3} \\ 1 & \frac{1}{3} \end{bmatrix}$ Ⓓ $\begin{bmatrix} 2 & -\frac{1}{3} \\ -1 & \frac{1}{3} \end{bmatrix}$

5. Which system corresponds to the matrix equation shown below?
$\begin{bmatrix} -42 & 76 \\ 38 & 17 \end{bmatrix}\begin{bmatrix} x \\ y \end{bmatrix} = \begin{bmatrix} -174 \\ 2473 \end{bmatrix}$

   Ⓐ $-42x + 38y = -174$
   $76x + 17y = 2473$

   Ⓑ $-42x + 17y = -174$
   $76x + 38y = 2473$

   Ⓒ $-42x + 76y = -174$
   $38x + 17y = 2473$

   Ⓓ $-42x + 76y = 2473$
   $38x + 17y = -174$

Short Response

6. Use an inverse matrix to find the solution of the following linear system.

   $x + 2y = -3$
   $2x - y = 4$

Extended Response

7. What is the area of a triangle with vertices $(-3, 8)$, $(1, 5)$, and $(6, -2)$?

Chapter Standardized Test 5A

Multiple Choice

1. What are the x-intercepts of the graph of the function $y = -3(x - 2)(x + 7)$?
   - Ⓐ 2 and −7
   - Ⓑ −2 and 7
   - Ⓒ −6 and 21
   - Ⓓ 6 and −21

2. What is a correct factorization of $4x^2 + 14x - 8$?
   - Ⓐ $(2x - 1)(2x + 4)$
   - Ⓑ $2(2x + 1)(x - 4)$
   - Ⓒ $2(x + 4)(2x - 1)$
   - Ⓓ $2(2x + 4)(x - 1)$

3. What are all solutions of $\frac{2}{3}(x - 3)^2 = 4$?
   - Ⓐ $-3 + \sqrt{6}$ and $-3 - \sqrt{6}$
   - Ⓑ $3 + \sqrt{6}$ and $3 - \sqrt{6}$
   - Ⓒ $-3 + 2\sqrt{3}$ and $-3 - 2\sqrt{3}$
   - Ⓓ $3 + 2\sqrt{3}$ and $3 - 2\sqrt{3}$

4. What is $2i + 3(1 - 4i) - 2(3 + 2i)$ written as a complex number in standard form?
   - Ⓐ $-3 - 6i$
   - Ⓑ $-1 - 16i$
   - Ⓒ $-3 - 14i$
   - Ⓓ $-1 - 2i$

5. What is the discriminant of $3x^2 - 14x + 9$?
   - Ⓐ −304
   - Ⓑ −94
   - Ⓒ 88
   - Ⓓ 2

6. What are all solutions of $x^2 + 8x - 6 = 0$?
   - Ⓐ $-4 + \sqrt{10}$ and $-4 - \sqrt{10}$
   - Ⓑ $4 + \sqrt{10}$ and $4 - \sqrt{10}$
   - Ⓒ $-8 + \sqrt{22}$ and $-8 - \sqrt{22}$
   - Ⓓ $-4 + \sqrt{22}$ and $-4 - \sqrt{22}$

7. What is the solution of $x^2 - x - 12 \geq 0$?
   - Ⓐ $-4 \leq x \leq 3$
   - Ⓑ $-3 \leq x \leq 4$
   - Ⓒ $x \leq -3$ or $x \geq 4$
   - Ⓓ $x \leq -4$ or $x \geq 3$

8. Which quadratic function represents a parabola whose graph has vertex $(-4, 2)$ and passes through the point $(3, 9)$?
   - Ⓐ $y = \frac{1}{7}(x - 4)^2 + 2$
   - Ⓑ $y = \frac{1}{7}(x + 4)^2 + 2$
   - Ⓒ $y = -\frac{1}{7}(x + 4)^2 + 2$
   - Ⓓ $y = -\frac{1}{7}(x - 4)^2 + 2$

Short Response

9. Solve $x^2 - 12x + 5 = 0$ by completing the square.

Extended Response

10. Plot the complex numbers below in the complex plane. Then give the absolute value of each complex number.

    $2 + 3i$
    $-1 - i$
    $-4 + 4i$
    $2 - 2i$

Chapter Standardized Test 5B

Multiple Choice

1. What are the x-intercepts of the graph of the function $y = \frac{1}{2}(x-4)(x+2)$?
   - Ⓐ 2 and −4
   - Ⓑ −2 and 4
   - Ⓒ 1 and −2
   - Ⓓ −1 and 2

2. What is a correct factorization of $3x^2 + 11x - 20$?
   - Ⓐ $(3x - 5)(x + 4)$
   - Ⓑ $(3x + 5)(x - 4)$
   - Ⓒ $(3x + 4)(x - 5)$
   - Ⓓ $(3x - 4)(x + 5)$

3. What are all solutions of $\frac{3}{4}(x+1)^2 = 9$?
   - Ⓐ $-1 + 2\sqrt{3}$ and $-1 - 2\sqrt{3}$
   - Ⓑ $-1 + \frac{3}{2}\sqrt{3}$ and $-1 - \frac{3}{2}\sqrt{3}$
   - Ⓒ $1 + 2\sqrt{3}$ and $1 - 2\sqrt{3}$
   - Ⓓ $1 + \frac{3}{2}\sqrt{3}$ and $1 - \frac{3}{2}\sqrt{3}$

4. What is $8(2 - 3i) + 2(4 + 2i) - 6$ written as a complex number in standard form?
   - Ⓐ $18 - 20i$
   - Ⓑ $14 - 20i$
   - Ⓒ $24 - 12i$
   - Ⓓ $20 - 12i$

5. What is the discriminant of $5x^2 + 17x - 9$?
   - Ⓐ 72
   - Ⓑ 109
   - Ⓒ 244
   - Ⓓ 469

6. What are all solutions of $x^2 - 10x + 3 = 0$?
   - Ⓐ $-5 + \sqrt{28}$ and $-5 - \sqrt{28}$
   - Ⓑ $5 + \sqrt{28}$ and $5 - \sqrt{28}$
   - Ⓒ $-5 + \sqrt{22}$ and $-5 - \sqrt{22}$
   - Ⓓ $5 + \sqrt{22}$ and $5 - \sqrt{22}$

7. What is the solution of $x^2 - 4x - 5 < 0$?
   - Ⓐ $x < -1$ or $x > 5$
   - Ⓑ $x < -5$ or $x > 1$
   - Ⓒ $-1 < x < 5$
   - Ⓓ $-5 < x < 1$

8. Which quadratic function represents a parabola whose graph has vertex (6, 1) and passes through the point (4, 9)?
   - Ⓐ $y = 2(x + 6)^2 + 1$
   - Ⓑ $y = 2(x - 6)^2 + 1$
   - Ⓒ $y = \frac{1}{2}(x + 6)^2 + 1$
   - Ⓓ $y = \frac{1}{2}(x - 6)^2 + 1$

Short Response

9. Solve $x^2 - 14x + 9 = 0$ by completing the square.

Extended Response

10. Plot the complex numbers below in a complex plane. Then give the absolute value of each complex number.

    $4i$
    $-2 - i$
    $-1 + 2i$
    $3 - 4i$

Chapter Standardized Test 6A

Multiple Choice

1. What is a simplified form of the expression $\dfrac{3x^{-2}y^4}{(6xy)^2}$?

   A $\dfrac{y^2}{12}$ **B** $\dfrac{y^2}{12x^4}$ **C** $\dfrac{y^2}{2}$ **D** $\dfrac{y^2}{2x^4}$

2. Which correctly describes the end behavior of $f(x) = 2x^3 - x^4 + 8x$?

   A $f(x) \to +\infty$ as $x \to -\infty$,
   $f(x) \to +\infty$ as $x \to +\infty$

   B $f(x) \to -\infty$ as $x \to -\infty$,
   $f(x) \to -\infty$ as $x \to +\infty$

   C $f(x) \to +\infty$ as $x \to -\infty$,
   $f(x) \to -\infty$ as $x \to +\infty$

   D $f(x) \to -\infty$ as $x \to -\infty$,
   $f(x) \to +\infty$ as $x \to +\infty$

3. What is the product $(x^2 - 6x + 4)(2x + 3)$?

   A $2x^3 - 5x^2 + 10x + 12$
   B $2x^3 - 5x^2 - 10x + 12$
   C $2x^3 - 9x^2 - 10x + 12$
   D $2x^3 - 9x^2 + 10x + 12$

4. What are the solutions of the equation $x^3 + 4x^2 - x = 4$?

   A $-4, -1, 1$ **B** $-1, 1, 4$
   C $-2, 1, 2$ **D** $-2, -1, 2$

5. What is the quotient $(x^3 + 2x^2 - 5x + 12) \div (x + 4)$?

   A $x^2 + 2x + 3$ **B** $x^2 - 2x + 3$
   C $x^2 - 2x - 3$ **D** $x^2 + 2x - 3$

6. What are the rational zeros of $f(x) = 2x^3 - 3x^2 - 32x - 15$?

   A $-\dfrac{3}{2}, -\dfrac{1}{2}, 1$ **B** $\dfrac{1}{2}, \dfrac{5}{2}, 3$
   C $-\dfrac{3}{2}, -1, 5$ **D** $-3, -\dfrac{1}{2}, 5$

7. What are the zeros of the polynomial function $f(x) = 2x^3 + 3x^2 + 8x + 12$?

   A $-\dfrac{3}{2}, -2i, 2i$ **B** $-\dfrac{3}{2}i, -2i, 2i$
   C $-3, -2i, 2i$ **D** $-3, i, -i$

8. What are the turning points of the graph of $f(x) = x^3 - 3x^2 - 9x + 4$?

   A $(1, -7)$ and $(3, -23)$
   B $(-1, 9)$ and $(3, -23)$
   C $(-1, 9)$ and $(-3, -77)$
   D $(1, -7)$ and $(-3, -77)$

9. What is the quotient $(4x^3 - 2x^2 + 6x - 2) \div (x + 1)$?

   A $-4x^2 + 2x + 4 - \dfrac{6}{x+1}$

   B $4x^2 - 6x + 12 - \dfrac{14}{x+1}$

   C $4x^2 - 6x - 12 + \dfrac{14}{x+1}$

   D $4x^2 + 6x - 12 + \dfrac{6}{x+1}$

Short Response

10. What is the degree of the polynomial function that fits the data?

x	1	2	3	4	5	6
f(x)	6	3	4	9	18	31

Extended Response

11. Use intercepts to graph the function $f(x) = \dfrac{1}{6}(x + 3)(x - 2)(x)$.

Chapter Standardized Test 6B

Multiple Choice

1. What is a simplified form of the expression $\dfrac{(3x^3y)^2}{12x^{-2}y^2}$?

   (A) $\dfrac{3x^8}{4}$ (B) $\dfrac{x^8}{4}$ (C) $\dfrac{3x^4}{4}$ (D) $\dfrac{x}{4y}$

2. Which correctly describes the end behavior of $f(x) = -x^3 + 17x^2 + 9$?

   (A) $f(x) \to +\infty$ as $x \to -\infty$,
   $f(x) \to +\infty$ as $x \to +\infty$

   (B) $f(x) \to -\infty$ as $x \to -\infty$,
   $f(x) \to -\infty$ as $x \to +\infty$

   (C) $f(x) \to +\infty$ as $x \to -\infty$,
   $f(x) \to -\infty$ as $x \to +\infty$

   (D) $f(x) \to -\infty$ as $x \to -\infty$,
   $f(x) \to +\infty$ as $x \to +\infty$

3. What is the product $(3x^2 + x - 5)(2x - 1)$?

   (A) $6x^3 + 5x^2 - 9x + 5$
   (B) $6x^3 - x^2 - 9x + 5$
   (C) $6x^3 + 5x^2 + 11x + 5$
   (D) $6x^3 - x^2 - 11x + 5$

4. What are the solutions of the equation $x^3 + 3x^2 - 4x = 12$?

   (A) $-4, 3, -4$ (B) $-3, -2, 2$
   (C) $-3, -1, 1$ (D) $-3, -1, 3$

5. What is the quotient $(x^3 - 5x^2 - 18x + 28) \div (x - 7)$?

   (A) $x^2 + 2x + 4$ (B) $x^2 + 2x - 4$
   (C) $x^2 - 2x - 4$ (D) $x^2 - 2x + 4$

6. What are all the rational zeros of $f(x) = 2x^3 + x^2 - 12x + 9$?

   (A) $-3, 1, \dfrac{3}{2}$ (B) $-\dfrac{1}{2}, \dfrac{3}{2}, 3$
   (C) $-3, \dfrac{1}{2}, \dfrac{3}{2}$ (D) $-3, -\dfrac{1}{2}, 5$

7. What are all the zeros of the polynomial function $f(x) = x^3 - x^2 + 9x - 9$?

   (A) $-1, -3i, 3i$ (B) $3, -i, i$
   (C) $1, -3i, 3i$ (D) $-3, -i, i$

8. What are the turning points of the graph of $f(x) = x^3 - 12x + 7$?

   (A) $(-2, -9)$ and $(2, 23)$
   (B) $(-2, 23)$ and $(2, -9)$
   (C) $(-2, 24)$ and $(2, -5)$
   (D) $(-2, -5)$ and $(2, 24)$

9. What is the quotient $(5x^3 + 3x^2 + 4x - 1) \div (x - 2)$?

   (A) $5x^2 - 7x + 18 - \dfrac{37}{x-2}$

   (B) $5x^2 - 7x + 18 + \dfrac{37}{x-2}$

   (C) $5x^2 + 13x + 30 + \dfrac{59}{x-2}$

   (D) $5x^2 + 13x + 30 - \dfrac{59}{x-2}$

Short Response

10. What is the degree of the polynomial function that fits the data?

x	1	2	3	4	5	6
$f(x)$	-3	2	13	30	53	82

Extended Response

11. Use intercepts to graph the function $f(x) = \dfrac{1}{4}(x + 2)(x - 4)(x - 1)$.

Name _____   Date _____

Building Test-Taking Skills

For use after Chapters 4–6

Scoring Rubric

Full credit
- answer is correct, *and*
- work or reasoning is included

Partial credit
- answer is correct, but reasoning is incorrect, *or*
- answer is incorrect, but reasoning is correct

No credit
- no answer is given, *or*
- answer makes no sense

Strategies for Answering
Short Response Questions

Problem

You work for your uncle this summer. He pays you $20 on your first day. Each day after that, you will get a raise. You can choose from 2 payment plans. With Plan A, you earn a $5 raise each day. With Plan B, you earn a 20% raise each day. Which plan is a better deal?

Full credit solution

Plan B is a better deal if you work more than 5 days.

Data are used to justify the solution.

Day	1	2	3	4	5	6
Plan A pay	20.00	25.00	30.00	35.00	40.00	45.00
Plan A total	20.00	45.00	75.00	110.00	150.00	195.00
Plan B pay	20.00	24.00	28.80	34.56	41.47	49.76
Plan B total	20.00	44.00	72.80	107.36	148.83	198.59

The question is answered clearly and in complete sentences.

Plan A is better if you work 5 days or less, but Plan B is better if you work more than 5 days. By day 6, the pay with a 20% increase is more than the pay with a $5 raise, so it will continue to be the better plan.

Partial credit solution

I think Plan B is better than Plan A.

The calculations are correct.

Day	1	2	3	4	5	6
Plan A	20.00	25.00	30.00	35.00	40.00	45.00
Plan B	20.00	24.00	28.80	34.56	41.47	49.76

The reasoning is faulty, because the total amount earned was not considered.

The first 4 days, Plan A is better. The next 2 days, Plan B is better. By day 5 Plan B pays you more money, so it is the better plan.

Building Test-Taking Skills *continued*

For use after Chapters 4–6

Partial credit solution

Plan A is better. The table shows that over the first four days, Plan A pays out $2.64 more than Plan B.

- The data do not include information past Day 4. So, the answer is incorrect.
- The data are calculated correctly.

Day	1	2	3	4
Plan A	20.00	25.00	30.00	35.00
Plan B	20.00	24.00	28.80	34.56
Difference	0	1.00	1.20	0.44

No credit solution

Plan A is better.

- The answer is incorrect.
- The data are not calculated correctly.

Day	1	2	3	4
Plan A	20.00	25.00	30.00	35.00
Plan B	20.00	24.00	26.00	28.00

Your turn now

Score each solution to the short response question below as *full credit, partial credit,* or *no credit.* Explain your reasoning.

Watch Out! Be sure to explain your reasoning clearly.

Problem

The Spiff travels 226.8 miles on 14 gallons of gas. The Flyte travels 280 miles on 17.5 gallons of gas. Which car is more fuel efficient?

1. The Spiff is the more fuel efficient car because it gets 16.2 miles per gallon. The Flyte gets 16 miles per gallon.

2. The Flyte gets 16 miles per gallon, because $280 \div 17.5 = 16$. The Spiff gets 16.2 miles per gallon, because $226.8 \div 14 = 16.2$. The more fuel efficient car gets a greater number of miles per gallon. Because 16.2 is greater than 16, the Spiff is more fuel efficient.

Practicing Test-Taking Skills
For use after Chapters 4–6

Short Response

1. The point $(-2, 3)$ represents $-2 + 3i$. What are the coordinates of the point that represents $i(-2 + 3i) - (4 - 5i)$? Explain your reasoning.

2. Samantha has $5000 to invest in accounts paying the interest rates shown at the right. She expects to invest in account A twice as much as she invests in account B and earn $200 in interest. How much will she invest in each account? Round to dollars and cents.

Account	Rate
A	3%
B	4%
C	5%

3. The product of three consecutive integers with x being the smallest can be represented by $x(x + 1)(x + 2)$. Prove that there are no three consecutive integers whose product is 1000.

4. Jada knows that the area of a rectangle is 56 square feet and that the length is one foot more than the width. What are the dimensions of a rectangle whose length and width are twice those of the original rectangle?

5. A rectangular prism has dimensions x, $x + 1$, and $x + 2$. What are simplified expressions for the surface area and volume of the prism?

6. The equation $\begin{bmatrix} 1 & 2 \\ 0 & 1 \end{bmatrix} \begin{bmatrix} x \\ y \end{bmatrix} = \begin{bmatrix} x' \\ y' \end{bmatrix}$ represents a transformation of the plane. The point $P(x, y)$ is transformed to the point $P'(x', y')$. A square has vertices $O(0, 0)$, $A(0, 3)$, $B(3, 3)$, and $C(3, 0)$. Find the images of these points under the transformation. Identify the quadrilateral that results.

7. The data below represent a linear function. Write an equation for y as a function of x. Then write an equation for x as a function of y.

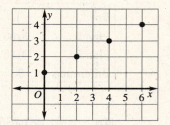

8. The data below represent temperature data (degrees Fahrenheit) gathered over a one-week period. Each temperature in the location was taken at noon.

d	1	2	3	4	5	6	7
t	71.2	71.8	71.9	72.3	72.7	73.2	73.9

   Verify that $t = 0.02d^2 + 0.25d + 71$ is a reasonable quadratic model of the data. Use the model to predict the noon temperature on day 10.

9. Two vertices of a square with horizontal and vertical sides are represented by $3 + 2i$ and $3 - 3i$. Each quadrant contains one vertex of the square.

   Graph the square in a coordinate plane.

   Write complex numbers for the four vertices.

   Find the perimeter of the square.

10. Lauren wants to make a flag whose length is 2.5 feet more than the width. She also wants the flag to have an area of 56 square feet.

    Can she make the flag she wants? Justify your answer.

    How does knowledge of quadratic equations help? How does a graph help?

Cumulative Practice
For use after Chapters 4–6

Chapter 4

Multiple Choice In Exercises 1–4, choose the letter of the correct answer.

1. What is the solution of the matrix equation for x and y? *(Lesson 4.1)*
$$\begin{bmatrix} 4 & x \\ x+y & y \end{bmatrix} + \begin{bmatrix} 3 & x+y \\ -2x & -y \end{bmatrix} = \begin{bmatrix} 7 & 1 \\ 8 & 0 \end{bmatrix}$$

   A $(1, 0)$
   B $\left(-2\frac{1}{3}, 5\frac{2}{3}\right)$
   C $\left(4\frac{1}{3}, 4\frac{2}{3}\right)$
   D $\left(2\frac{1}{3}, 3\frac{2}{3}\right)$

2. What is the area of a triangle with vertices $A(4, -2)$, $B(7, 3)$, and $C(1, 8)$? *(Lesson 4.3)*

   A 16 square units
   B 18.5 square units
   C 22.5 square units
   D 65 square units

3. Solve the matrix equation for the matrix X. *(Lesson 4.4)*
$$\begin{bmatrix} -5 & 3 \\ 3 & 2 \end{bmatrix} X = \begin{bmatrix} -6 & 1 \\ 3 & 7 \end{bmatrix}$$

   A $\begin{bmatrix} \frac{21}{19} & -1 \\ -\frac{3}{19} & -2 \end{bmatrix}$
   B $\begin{bmatrix} \frac{21}{19} & 1 \\ -\frac{3}{19} & 2 \end{bmatrix}$

   C $\begin{bmatrix} 1 & \frac{21}{19} \\ 2 & -\frac{3}{19} \end{bmatrix}$
   D $\begin{bmatrix} -1 & -\frac{21}{19} \\ -2 & \frac{3}{19} \end{bmatrix}$

4. What is the solution of the linear system? Use an inverse matrix. *(Lesson 4.5)*
$$x - 2y + z = -14$$
$$y - 2z = 7$$
$$2x + 3y - z = -1$$

   A $(-2, 3, 0)$
   B $(-6, -1, 0)$
   C $(-2, -1, -2)$
   D $(-6, 3, -2)$

5. **Short Response** Perform the indicated matrix operations. Show your work. *(Lessons 4.1, 4.2)*
$$\begin{bmatrix} 4 & -2 \\ 3 & -5 \end{bmatrix} \begin{bmatrix} 3 & 0 \\ 2 & -1 \end{bmatrix} + 3\begin{bmatrix} 1 & 4 \\ 9 & -3 \end{bmatrix}$$

6. **Extended Response** Teams of students can put on skits, do demonstrations, or show a video at a performance. The director wants to schedule this year's performance and needs to know how long each part typically takes. The table shows information from previous years. *(Lessons 4.3, 4.5)*

Skits	Demos	Videos	Total Time
1	2	1	47 min
3	4	1	91 min
5	1	3	115 min

   a. Write a system of equations to model the situation.

   b. Write the system as a system of matrices.

   c. Solve the system to find how long each part typically takes.

Cumulative Practice continued

For use after Chapters 4–6

Chapter 5

Multiple Choice In Exercises 7–14, choose the letter of the correct answer.

7. What is the vertex of the graph of $y = \frac{1}{3}x^2 - 2x + 5$? (Lesson 5.1)

    Ⓐ $(3, -4)$ Ⓑ $(1, -4)$
    Ⓒ $(3, 2)$ Ⓓ $(1, 5)$

8. What is a factorization of $2x^2 - x - 21$? (Lesson 5.2)

    Ⓐ $(2x + 7)(x - 3)$ Ⓑ $(2x + 7)(x + 3)$
    Ⓒ $(2x - 7)(x - 3)$ Ⓓ $(2x - 7)(x + 3)$

9. What are the solutions of $(x - 4)^2 = 15$? (Lesson 5.3)

    Ⓐ $4 + \sqrt{15}$ and $4 - \sqrt{15}$
    Ⓑ $4 + \sqrt{15}$ and $-4 + \sqrt{15}$
    Ⓒ $2 + \sqrt{15}$ and $2 - \sqrt{15}$
    Ⓓ $2 + \sqrt{15}$ and $-2 + \sqrt{15}$

10. What are the solutions of $4x^2 + 9 = 1$? (Lesson 5.4)

    Ⓐ $2i$ and $-2i$
    Ⓑ $\sqrt{2} + i$ and $\sqrt{2} - i$
    Ⓒ $i\sqrt{2}$ and $-i\sqrt{2}$
    Ⓓ $\sqrt{2}$ and $-\sqrt{2}$

11. What is the minimum value of $f(x) = \frac{1}{2}x^2 - 3x + 8$? (Lesson 5.5)

    Ⓐ 3 Ⓑ $3\frac{1}{2}$ Ⓒ $5\frac{1}{2}$ Ⓓ 8

12. At how many points does the graph of $y = -5x^2 + 3x - 1$ intersect the x-axis? (Lesson 5.6)

    Ⓐ 0 Ⓑ 1 Ⓒ 2 Ⓓ 3

13. What is the solution of $-x^2 + x \geq -20$? (Lesson 5.7)

    Ⓐ $x \leq -4$ or $x \geq 5$
    Ⓑ $-4 \leq x \leq 5$
    Ⓒ $x \leq -5$ or $x \geq 4$
    Ⓓ $-5 \leq x \leq 4$

14. Which quadratic function is graphed below? (Lesson 5.8)

    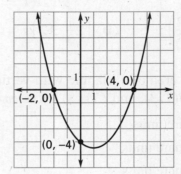

    Ⓐ $y = \frac{1}{2}(x - 4)(x + 2)$
    Ⓑ $y = \frac{1}{2}(x + 4)(x - 2)$
    Ⓒ $y = (x - 4)(x + 2)$
    Ⓓ $y = (x + 4)(x - 2)$

15. **Short Response** What is the solution of $x^2 + 9x + 21 = -3x - 15$? (Lesson 5.2)

16. **Extended Response** Graph the system of quadratic inequalities. List three points that are solutions of the system. (Lesson 5.7)

    $y \leq -\frac{1}{2}x^2 + 2x$

    $y \geq x^2 - 6x + 5$

Cumulative Practice *continued*
For use after Chapters 4–6

Chapter 6

Multiple Choice In Exercises 17–25, choose the letter of the correct answer.

17. What is a simplified form of $(3x^3y^2)^4(2y)^{-3}$? *(Lesson 6.1)*
    - Ⓐ $\frac{3}{2}x^{12}y^5$
    - Ⓑ $\frac{3}{2}x^7y^3$
    - Ⓒ $\frac{81}{8}x^{12}y^5$
    - Ⓓ $\frac{81}{8}x^7y^3$

18. What is the value of $f(x) = -2x^4 + 5x^3 - 7x^2 + x - 1$ when $x = -2$? *(Lesson 6.2)*
    - Ⓐ -103
    - Ⓑ -87
    - Ⓒ -23
    - Ⓓ -19

19. What is the difference of the polynomials? *(Lesson 6.3)*
    $(4x^2 - 3x^3 + 8x - 1) - (6x^3 + 5x - 4)$
    - Ⓐ $-2x^3 - 3x^2 + 3x + 3$
    - Ⓑ $-9x^3 + 4x^2 + 3x + 3$
    - Ⓒ $10x^3 - 3x^2 + 13x - 5$
    - Ⓓ $3x^3 + 4x^2 + 13x - 5$

20. What are the solutions of $x^3 - 5x^2 + 2x = 4x^2 + 3x - 9$? *(Lesson 6.4)*
    - Ⓐ $-1, 1, 9$
    - Ⓑ $-1, -3, 3$
    - Ⓒ $-9, -1, 1$
    - Ⓓ $-3, 1, 3$

21. One zero of $f(x) = x^3 - 5x^2 - 22x + 56$ is 7. What are the other zeros of the function? *(Lesson 6.5)*
    - Ⓐ $1, 8$
    - Ⓑ $-1, -8$
    - Ⓒ $-2, 4$
    - Ⓓ $-4, 2$

22. What are the rational zeros of $f(x) = 3x^3 - 14x^2 - 7x + 10$? *(Lesson 6.6)*
    - Ⓐ $-5, -1, \frac{2}{3}$
    - Ⓑ $-1, \frac{2}{3}, 5$
    - Ⓒ $-2, -1, 5$
    - Ⓓ $-1, 2, 5$

23. How many solutions does the equation $y = x^5 - 6x^3 + 4x$ have? *(Lesson 6.7)*
    - Ⓐ 3
    - Ⓑ 4
    - Ⓒ 5
    - Ⓓ 6

24. What is the greatest number of turning points the graph of $y = 3x^4 + 5x$ can have? *(Lesson 6.8)*
    - Ⓐ 2
    - Ⓑ 3
    - Ⓒ 4
    - Ⓓ 5

25. What is the degree of the polynomial function that fits the data? *(Lesson 6.9)*

x	1	2	3	4	5	6
$f(x)$	5	21	23	14	-3	-25

    - Ⓐ 2
    - Ⓑ 3
    - Ⓒ 4
    - Ⓓ 5

26. **Short Response** Write a polynomial function of least degree that has real coefficients, a leading coefficient of 1, and -3, 4, and $2 - i$ as zeros. *(Lesson 6.7)*

27. **Extended Response** What is the end behavior of the graphs of $y = 4x^3 - 3x^2$ and $y = -4x^4 - 3x^2$? Explain the differences. *(Lesson 6.2)*

Chapter Standardized Test 7A

Multiple Choice

1. What is the value of $625^{3/4}$?
   - **A** 5
   - **B** $5\sqrt{5}$
   - **C** 25
   - **D** 125

2. What is a simplified form of the expression $(-8x^2y^{-6})^{1/3}$?
   - **A** $2x^6y^2$
   - **B** $2x^{2/3}y^{-2}$
   - **C** $-2x^{2/3}y^{-2}$
   - **D** $-2x^6y^3$

3. If $f(x) = -x^2$ and $g(x) = 2x - 3$, what is $g(f(x))$?
   - **A** $-2x^2 - 3$
   - **B** $-2x^3 + 3x^2$
   - **C** $-x^2 + 2x - 3$
   - **D** $-4x^2 + 12x - 9$

4. What is an equation for the inverse of the relation $f(x) = 9 - 3x$?
   - **A** $f^{-1}(x) = \frac{1}{3}x - 3$
   - **B** $f^{-1}(x) = -\frac{1}{3}x + 3$
   - **C** $f^{-1}(x) = -x + 3$
   - **D** $f^{-1}(x) = 9x - 3$

5. What is the range of the function $y = -\sqrt{x+1} - 2$?
   - **A** $x \geq -1$
   - **B** $y \leq -2$
   - **C** $x \leq -1$
   - **D** $y \geq -2$

6. What is the solution of $\sqrt{2x+7} - 1 = 2$?
   - **A** -1
   - **B** 1
   - **C** $\frac{3}{2}$
   - **D** 3

7. The box-and-whisker plot shown could represent which set of data?

   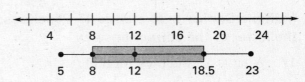

   - **A** 5, 5, 6, 8, 8, 8, 9, 10, 10, 11, 13, 15, 15, 16, 18, 19, 21, 21, 23, 23
   - **B** 5, 6, 7, 7, 8, 9, 9, 10, 11, 12, 12, 13, 15, 15, 15, 16, 16, 17, 22, 23
   - **C** 5, 5, 6, 6, 7, 9, 10, 11, 12, 13, 13, 14, 18, 18, 18, 19, 21, 22, 22, 23
   - **D** 5, 6, 6, 6, 8, 10, 11, 11, 12, 12, 12, 13, 13, 14, 15, 18, 19, 19, 20, 23

Short Response

8. If $f(x) = x^2 - x + 1$ and $g(x) = 2x - 3$, what is $f(g(x))$? What is $g(f(x))$?

Extended Response

9. The data set shows the high temperatures, in degrees Fahrenheit, recorded at a school for one month.

   64, 64, 65, 66, 66, 68, 68, 68, 69, 69, 70, 70, 71, 72, 72, 72, 72, 72, 73, 73, 74, 75, 75, 76, 76, 77, 78, 80, 80, 82

   Find the range, mean, median, and mode of the data set. Make a box-and-whisker plot of the data.

Chapter Standardized Test 7B

Multiple Choice

1. What is the value of $81^{3/4}$?

   Ⓐ 3   Ⓑ 9   Ⓒ 27   Ⓓ 243

2. What is a simplified form of the expression $(3^{-4}a^6b^3)^{1/2}$?

   Ⓐ $-81a^3b^{3/2}$ Ⓑ $\frac{1}{9}a^3b^{3/2}$
   Ⓒ $-12a^2b^6$ Ⓓ $-9a^3b^{2/3}$

3. If $f(x) = 4x + 3$ and $g(x) = -2x - 5$, what is $g(f(x))$?

   Ⓐ $-8x - 17$
   Ⓑ $-8x - 11$
   Ⓒ $2x - 2$
   Ⓓ $-8x^2 - 26x - 15$

4. What is an equation for the inverse of the relation $f(x) = 6x + 12$?

   Ⓐ $f^{-1}(x) = \frac{1}{6}x - 2$
   Ⓑ $f^{-1}(x) = \frac{1}{6}x + 2$
   Ⓒ $f^{-1}(x) = -\frac{1}{6}x - 2$
   Ⓓ $f^{-1}(x) = -\frac{1}{6}x + 2$

5. What is the range of the function $y = 3\sqrt{2x - 5} + 4$?

   Ⓐ $x \leq \frac{5}{2}$ Ⓑ $x \geq \frac{5}{2}$
   Ⓒ $y \leq 4$ Ⓓ $y \geq 4$

6. What is the solution of $\sqrt{3x + 16} + 1 = 3$?

   Ⓐ -4 Ⓑ -2
   Ⓒ $-\frac{16}{3}$ Ⓓ 4

7. The box-and-whisker plot shown could represent which set of data?

   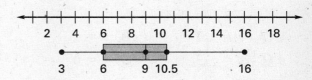

   Ⓐ 3, 3, 6, 6, 6, 6, 6, 7, 7, 8, 8, 8, 9, 10, 10, 11, 12, 13, 15, 16
   Ⓑ 3, 4, 5, 5, 5, 7, 7, 8, 8, 9, 9, 9, 10, 10, 11, 11, 11, 12, 13, 16
   Ⓒ 3, 3, 5, 6, 6, 6, 7, 7, 8, 9, 9, 9, 10, 10, 10, 11, 11, 13, 14, 16
   Ⓓ 3, 5, 5, 6, 7, 7, 7, 8, 8, 8, 9, 9, 10, 10, 11, 11, 12, 13, 16, 16

Short Response

8. If $f(x) = 2x^2 - x + 5$ and $g(x) = -3x + 4$, what is $f(g(x))$? What is $g(f(x))$?

Extended Response

9. The data set shows the high temperatures, in degrees Fahrenheit, recorded at a school for one month.

   16, 18, 19, 21, 21, 21, 21, 22, 22, 23, 23, 23, 23, 23, 24, 25, 25, 28, 28, 29, 29, 32, 32, 33, 35, 37, 37, 40, 40, 45

   Find the range, mean, median, and mode of the data set. Make a box-and-whisker plot of the data.

Name _____ Date _____

Chapter Standardized Test 8A

Multiple Choice

1. What is the asymptote of the graph of $y = -3 \cdot 2^x + 2$?

   A $y = -2$ **B** $y = 2$
   C $x = -3$ **D** $x = 0$

2. What is the range of the function $y = 4\left(\dfrac{1}{3}\right)^x - 1$?

   A $y \leq -1$ **B** $y < -1$
   C $y \geq -1$ **D** $y > -1$

3. What is the simplified form of the expression $2(e^{3x})^4$?

   A $2e^{12x}$ **B** $2e^{7x}$
   C $8e^{7x}$ **D** $16e^{12x}$

4. What is the exponential form of $\log_{16} 4 = \dfrac{1}{2}$?

   A $16^4 = \dfrac{1}{2}$
   B $16^{1/2} = 4$
   C $\left(\dfrac{1}{2}\right)^4 = 16$
   D $4^2 = 16$

5. What is the simplified form of the expression $2 \log 4 + 2 \log 3 - 3 \log 2$?

   A $\log 8$ **B** $\log 9$
   C $\log 18$ **D** $\log 22$

6. What is the solution of the equation $\log_2 (4x - 3) = \log_2 (x + 9)$?

   A 1 **B** 3 **C** 4 **D** 6

7. What is y written as a function of x?

   $\ln y = 2x - 1$

   A $y = 0.368e^{2x}$ **B** $y = e^{2x} - 1$
   C $y = 2.718e^{2x}$ **D** $y = e^{2x} - e$

8. What are the asymptotes of the graph of $y = \dfrac{4}{1 + 3e^{-0.2x}}$?

   A $y = 0.2, y = 4$
   B $y = -3, y = 4$
   C $y = -3, y = 0$
   D $y = 0, y = 4$

Short Response

9. Find a power function of the form $y = ax^b$ whose graph passes through (2, 9) and (4, 27).

Extended Response

10. Use the table of values to draw a scatter plot of $\ln y$ versus $\ln x$. Then find an exponential model for the data.

x	0.5	1.0	1.5	2.0	2.5	3.0
y	0.435	1.000	1.627	2.297	3.003	3.737

Chapter Standardized Test 8B

Multiple Choice

1. What is the asymptote of the graph of $y = 1.5 \cdot 5^x - 4$?
   - Ⓐ $x = 0$
   - Ⓑ $x = 4$
   - Ⓒ $y = -4$
   - Ⓓ $y = 4$

2. What is the range of the function $y = 6.8\left(\dfrac{2}{5}\right)^x + 3.2$?
   - Ⓐ $y \geq 3.2$
   - Ⓑ $y < 3.2$
   - Ⓒ $y \leq 3.2$
   - Ⓓ $y > 3.2$

3. What is the simplified form of the expression $e^{-2x} \cdot (3e^x)^3$?
   - Ⓐ $27e^x$
   - Ⓑ $27e^{-6x}$
   - Ⓒ $27e^{-x}$
   - Ⓓ $27e^{-5x}$

4. What is the exponential equation of $\log_{125} 5 = \dfrac{1}{3}$?
   - Ⓐ $5^3 = 125$
   - Ⓑ $125^{1/3} = 5$
   - Ⓒ $\left(\dfrac{1}{3}\right)^5 = 125$
   - Ⓓ $3^5 = 125$

5. What is the simplified form of the expression $3 \log 5 - 3 \log 2 + 2 \log 4$?
   - Ⓐ $\log 17$
   - Ⓑ $\log 29$
   - Ⓒ $\log 62.5$
   - Ⓓ $\log 250$

6. What is the solution of the equation $\log_{10}(3x - 5) = \log_{10}(4x - 3)$?
   - Ⓐ -2
   - Ⓑ -1
   - Ⓒ 1
   - Ⓓ 2

7. What is y written as a function of x?
   $\ln y = 3x + 4$
   - Ⓐ $y = e^{3x} + 4$
   - Ⓑ $y = 3e^x + 4$
   - Ⓒ $y = 54.6e^{3x}$
   - Ⓓ $y = 20.1e^{3x} + 4$

8. What are the asymptotes of the graph of $y = \dfrac{9}{1 + 5e^{-0.8x}}$?
   - Ⓐ $y = 0, y = 9$
   - Ⓑ $y = 5, y = 9$
   - Ⓒ $y = 0, y = 5$
   - Ⓓ $y = 6, y = 9$

Short Response

9. Find a power function of the form $y = ax^b$ whose graph passes through $(2, 4)$ and $(8, 27)$.

Extended Response

10. Use the table of values to draw a scatter plot of $\ln y$ versus $\ln x$. Then find an exponential model for the data.

x	0.5	1.0	1.5	2.0	2.5	3.0
y	0.177	1.000	2.756	5.657	9.882	15.588

Chapter Standardized Test 9A

Multiple Choice

1. The variable x varies inversely with y. When $x = 3$, $y = -6$. Which equation relates x and y?

   Ⓐ $y = -2x$

   Ⓑ $y = -\dfrac{18}{x}$

   Ⓒ $y = -\dfrac{12}{x} - 3$

   Ⓓ $y = -\dfrac{12}{x}$

2. Which function is graphed?

   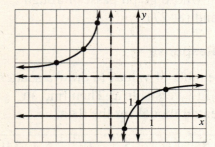

   Ⓐ $y = \dfrac{-8}{x+2} - 3$

   Ⓑ $y = \dfrac{-8}{x+2} + 3$

   Ⓒ $y = \dfrac{-4}{x+2} - 3$

   Ⓓ $y = \dfrac{-4}{x+2} + 3$

3. What are the x-intercepts of the graph of $y = \dfrac{x^2 - 3x - 10}{2x^2 + 10x + 8}$?

   Ⓐ -1 and -4

   Ⓑ 1 and 4

   Ⓒ 5 and -2

   Ⓓ 2 and -5

4. What is the product $\dfrac{x+4}{x^3 - 2x^2 - x + 2} \cdot (x^2 - 3x + 2)$?

   Ⓐ $\dfrac{x-1}{x+1}$ Ⓑ $\dfrac{x+4}{x+1}$

   Ⓒ $\dfrac{x+4}{x^2 - 1}$ Ⓓ $\dfrac{x-1}{x^2 + 1}$

5. What is the sum $\dfrac{5x}{4x^2 - 1} + \dfrac{2x+1}{3x}$?

   Ⓐ $\dfrac{8x^3 + 19x^2 - 2x - 1}{3x(4x^2 - 1)}$

   Ⓑ $\dfrac{4x^2 + 15x - 1}{3x(4x^2 - 1)}$

   Ⓒ $\dfrac{8x^3 + 2x^2 - 15x + 1}{3x(4x^2 - 1)}$

   Ⓓ $\dfrac{8x^2 + 2x - 1}{3x(4x^2 - 1)}$

6. What are all the solutions of $\dfrac{1}{x+2} = \dfrac{4x - 8}{x^2 + 3x + 44}$?

   Ⓐ $-4, 5$

   Ⓑ $-4, 3$

   Ⓒ $1, 3$

   Ⓓ $1, 5$

Short Response

7. Simplify $\dfrac{x^3 + 2x^2 - 8x}{x^2 + 5x - 14}$.

Extended Response

8. Graph the function $y = \dfrac{1}{x - 2} - 1$. State the domain and range.

Name _____ Date _____

Chapter Standardized Test 9B

Multiple Choice

1. The variable x varies inversely with y. When $x = 5$, $y = 10$. Which equation relates x and y?

   A $y = 2x$ **B** $y = \dfrac{30}{x} + 4$

   C $y = \dfrac{1}{2x}$ **D** $y = \dfrac{50}{x}$

2. Which function is graphed?

   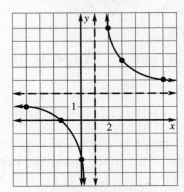

   A $y = \dfrac{5}{x-1} + 2$

   B $y = \dfrac{5}{x-1} - 2$

   C $y = \dfrac{8}{x-1} + 2$

   D $y = \dfrac{8}{x-1} - 2$

3. What are the x-intercepts of the graph of $y = \dfrac{x^2 - 7x - 8}{x^2 - 9}$?

   A -1 and 8
   B 1 and -8
   C -3 and 3
   D 8 and 9

4. What is the product $\dfrac{x}{x^2 + x - 30} \cdot (x^2 + 5x - 6)$?

   A $\dfrac{x-1}{x-5}$ **B** $\dfrac{x^2 - x}{x - 5}$

   C $\dfrac{x-1}{x+5}$ **D** $\dfrac{x^2 - 6x}{x + 5}$

5. What is the sum $\dfrac{x-7}{x^2 - 9} + \dfrac{x+3}{x^2 - 4x + 3}$?

   A $\dfrac{2(x+1)}{(x-3)(x+3)(x-1)}$

   B $\dfrac{4x^2 - 4x - 1}{(x-3)(x+3)(x-1)}$

   C $\dfrac{2(x^2 - x + 8)}{(x-3)(x+3)(x-1)}$

   D $\dfrac{x^2 - 8x - 2}{(x-3)(x+3)(x-1)}$

6. What are all the solutions of $\dfrac{x+1}{2x^2 - x - 7} = \dfrac{1}{x-1}$?

   A $-1, 3$
   B $-2, 3$
   C $-1, 4$
   D $-2, 4$

Short Response

7. Simplify $\dfrac{2x^2 + 11x - 21}{x^2 + 6x - 7}$.

Extended Response

8. Graph the function $y = \dfrac{1}{x+2} + 3$. State the domain and range.

Building Test-Taking Skills

For use after Chapters 7–9

Strategies for Answering
Context-Based Multiple Choice Questions

Some of the information you need to solve a context-based multiple choice question may appear in a table, a diagram, or a graph.

Problem 1

Ali plants a flower garden in a circle around a tree. The outer edge of the garden has twice the radius of the inner edge. Find the area of the flower garden.

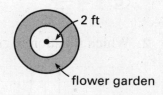

A. 12.56 ft²   **B.** 25.12 ft²   **C.** 37.68 ft²   **D.** 50.24 ft²

Solution

Read the problem carefully. Decide how you can use the information you are given to solve the problem.

1) You know that the radius of the inner circle is 2 feet and the radius of the outer circle is double the radius of the inner circle, or 4 feet.

Use the areas of both circles to find the area of the garden.

Find the areas of the two circles.

2) Area of inner circle:
    radius = 2 ft
    $A = \pi r^2$
    $= \pi \cdot 2^2$
    $= 4\pi$

 Area of outer circle:
    radius = 4 ft
    $A = \pi r^2$
    $= \pi \cdot 4^2$
    $= 16\pi$

Use the areas of the circles to find the area of the garden.

3) Area of garden = Area of outer circle − Area of inner circle
    $A = 16\pi - 4\pi$
       $= 12\pi$
       $\approx 12 \times 3.14$
       $= 37.68$

The area of the flower garden is about 37.68 ft².

The correct answer is C.

Check to see that the answer is reasonable.

4) Estimate that 16π is about 48 and 4π is about 12. Because 48 − 12 = 36, C is the most reasonable choice.

Building Test-Taking Skills continued

For use after Chapters 7–9

Problem 2

Jim walks diagonally across a field. Martha walks along its length and width. The rectangular field is 300 feet wide and 400 feet long. How many feet less does Jim walk than Martha?

A. 1200 feet   B. 700 feet   C. 500 feet   D. 200 feet

Solution

Read the problem carefully. Remember that the field is a rectangle.

1) Use the information in the problem to make a sketch.

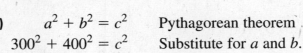

Use the Pythagorean theorem to find the length of Jim's path. Add to find the length of Martha's path.

2) $a^2 + b^2 = c^2$ Pythagorean theorem
$300^2 + 400^2 = c^2$ Substitute for a and b.
$250{,}000 = c^2$ Solve.
$500 = c$ Evaluate positive square root.

The length of Jim's path is 500 feet.
The length of Martha's path is $300 + 400 = 700$ feet.

Find the difference of the two distances.

3) Martha's distance − Jim's distance
$= 700 - 500$
$= 200$

Jim walks 200 feet less than Martha.   **The correct answer is D.**

Your turn now

Watch Out! Be sure that you know what question you are asked to answer. Some choices given may be intended to distract you.

1. In Problem 2, Jim and Martha both walk at the rate of 250 ft/min. How many minutes less does Jim walk than Martha?

   A. 0.2 min   B. 0.25 min   C. 0.8 min   D. 1.25 min

In Exercises 2–3, use the diagram.

2. What is the height of the building?

   A. 10 feet   B. 16 feet
   C. 20 feet   D. 40 feet

3. How long will the person's shadow be when the building's shadow is 14 feet long?

   A. 3 feet   B. 3.5 feet
   C. 4 feet   D. 7 feet

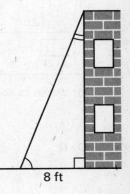

Practicing Test-Taking Skills
For use after Chapters 7–9

Multiple Choice

1. Suppose you invest the minimum amount in the account shown. What expression represents the amount in the account after 9 months?

   > 5% interest compounded yearly
   > $1000 minimum

   Ⓐ $1000(1.05)^9$ Ⓑ $1000\left(\frac{3}{4} \times 1.05\right)$
   Ⓒ $1000(1.05)^{3/4}$ Ⓓ $1000(1 + 0.5)^{3/4}$

2. A rectangular prism is filled with water weighing about 62.4 pounds per cubic foot. Which equation represents this statement?

   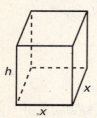

   Ⓐ $w = 62.4x^2h$ Ⓑ $w = \frac{62.4h}{x^2}$
   Ⓒ $w = \frac{62.4x^2}{h}$ Ⓓ $wx^2h = 62.4$

3. The two rectangles have the same ratio of length to width. What is the value of x?

   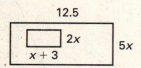

   Not drawn to scale

   Ⓐ 2, −2 Ⓑ 2
   Ⓒ 0 Ⓓ 2.5

4. The ratio of the lengths of the legs of a right triangle is 3 to 4. How long are the legs if the hypotenuse is 12?

   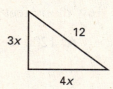

   Ⓐ 9 and 12 Ⓑ $\frac{9}{5}$ and $\frac{12}{5}$
   Ⓒ 12 and 16 Ⓓ $7\frac{1}{5}$ and $9\frac{3}{5}$

5. What is the ratio of the volume of the cube to the volume of the inscribed sphere?

   Ⓐ $\frac{2}{\pi}$ Ⓑ $\frac{3}{\pi}$ Ⓒ $\frac{4}{\pi}$ Ⓓ $\frac{6}{\pi}$

6. The tables below show exponential functions f and g. Which function h represents the composite function, f followed by g?

x	0	1	2	3
$f(x)$	1	2	4	8

x	0	1	2	3
$g(x)$	1	3	9	27

   Ⓐ $h(x) = 2^{3x}$ Ⓑ $h(x) = 2^{3^x}$
   Ⓒ $h(x) = 3^{2^x}$ Ⓓ $h(x) = 3^{2x}$

Name _____ Date _____

Cumulative Practice
For use after Chapters 7–9

Chapter 7

Multiple Choice In Exercises 1–7, choose the letter of the correct answer.

1. What are the solutions of $x^4 - 24 = 40$? *(Lesson 7.1)*

   Ⓐ $\pm 2\sqrt{2}$ Ⓑ ± 4
   Ⓒ ± 8 Ⓓ $\pm 4\sqrt{2}$

2. What is a simplified form of $2\sqrt{5} - \sqrt{45}$? *(Lesson 7.2)*

   Ⓐ $-7\sqrt{5}$ Ⓑ $-\sqrt{5}$
   Ⓒ $2\sqrt{5} - 3$ Ⓓ $2\sqrt{5} - 5\sqrt{3}$

3. What is the value of the expression $\dfrac{g(x)}{f(x)}$ when $f(x) = 8x^{3/2}$ and $g(x) = 2x^4$? *(Lesson 7.3)*

   Ⓐ $\dfrac{4}{x^{3/2}}$ Ⓑ $\dfrac{x^{3/2}}{4}$
   Ⓒ $\dfrac{4}{x^{5/2}}$ Ⓓ $\dfrac{x^{5/2}}{4}$

4. What is the inverse of the function $f(x) = 8x^3 - 13$? *(Lesson 7.4)*

   Ⓐ $f^{-1}(x) = \dfrac{\sqrt[3]{x+13}}{2}$

   Ⓑ $f^{-1}(x) = \sqrt[3]{x} + \dfrac{13}{8}$

   Ⓒ $f^{-1}(x) = \dfrac{\sqrt[3]{x} + \sqrt[3]{13}}{2}$

   Ⓓ $f^{-1}(x) = \dfrac{\sqrt[3]{x+13}}{8}$

5. What are the domain and range of the function $y = 4 - \sqrt{9x - 45}$? *(Lesson 7.5)*

   Ⓐ domain: $x \geq 5$ Ⓑ domain: $x \leq 5$
   range: $y \geq 4$ range: $y \geq 4$

   Ⓒ domain: $x \geq 5$ Ⓓ domain: $x \leq 5$
   range: $y \leq 4$ range: $y \leq 4$

6. What are all the solutions of $\sqrt{9x + 37} = x + 3$? *(Lesson 7.6)*

   Ⓐ $-4, 7$
   Ⓑ 7
   Ⓒ $-3, 0$
   Ⓓ -4

7. What is the median of the data set below? *(Lesson 7.7)*

   $-8, -6, -6, -2, 1, 1, 1, 2, 3, 3, 5, 5, 7, 9, 10$

   Ⓐ 1 Ⓑ 1.5 Ⓒ 1.67 Ⓓ 2

8. **Short Response** Let $f(x) = 4x^{3/2}$ and $g(x) = 6x^{1/2}$. Find $f(x) \cdot g(x)$, $\dfrac{f(x)}{g(x)}$, and $\dfrac{g(x)}{f(x)}$. *(Lesson 7.3)*

9. **Extended Response** Data about summer rainfalls (in inches) is given below. *(Lesson 7.7)*

   3.6, 3.7, 4.0, 4.1, 4.2, 4.4, 4.7, 4.7, 4.8, 4.9, 4.9, 5.0, 5.1, 5.1, 5.1, 5.3, 5.5, 5.5

   a. Find the mean of the data.
   b. Find the standard deviation of the data.
   c. Suppose that several dry summers with rainfalls of 0.9, 1.2, 1.3, 1.3, 1.4, and 1.7 inches were added to the data. Without calculating the new values, explain the effect this would have on the mean and standard deviation.

Algebra 2 49
North Carolina Standards Test Preparation and Practice

Cumulative Practice continued
For use after Chapters 7–9

Chapter 8

Multiple Choice In Exercises 10–17, choose the letter of the correct answer.

10. You deposit $10,000 into a CD earning 7% annual interest compounded quarterly. What is the balance after 8 years? *(Lesson 8.1)*

    Ⓐ $17,181.86 Ⓑ $17,422.13
    Ⓒ $17,505.79 Ⓓ $17,506.73

11. You buy a car for $18,000. Its value decreases by 14% each year. What is its value after 5 years? *(Lesson 8.2)*

    Ⓐ $8468 Ⓑ $9836
    Ⓒ $14,677 Ⓓ $34,657

12. Which function is an example of an exponential decay function? *(Lesson 8.3)*

    Ⓐ $y = 0.007e^{2.1x}$ Ⓑ $y = e^{1.5x}$
    Ⓒ $y = 1.5e^{3x}$ Ⓓ $y = 425e^{-0.8x}$

13. Which function is the inverse of $y = \log_5 (x + 1)$? *(Lesson 8.4)*

    Ⓐ $y = \log_{(x+1)} 5$ Ⓑ $y = (x + 1)^5$
    Ⓒ $y = 5^{x+1}$ Ⓓ $y = 5^x - 1$

14. What is an expanded form of $\log \frac{8b^3}{a^2}$? Assume a and b are positive. *(Lesson 8.5)*

    Ⓐ $8 \log 3b - \log 2a$
    Ⓑ $\log 8 + \log 3b - \log 2a$
    Ⓒ $\log 8 + 3 \log b - 2 \log a$
    Ⓓ $8 \log 3b - 8 \log 2a$

15. What is the solution of $e^{4x-1} - 3 = 7$? *(Lesson 8.6)*

    Ⓐ 0.826 Ⓑ 0.576
    Ⓒ 0.5 Ⓓ 0.326

16. The data in the table can be used to write an exponential function for y in terms of x. Which equation fits the data? *(Lesson 8.7)*

x	0	1	2	3	4
ln y	4.2	6.6	8.0	10.4	12.8

    Ⓐ $y = 11.0(66.7)^x$
    Ⓑ $y = 66.7(11.0)^x$
    Ⓒ $y = 4.2 + 2.4x$
    Ⓓ $y = 4.2e^{2.4x}$

17. What is the y-value at the point of maximum growth in the graph of the logistic function $y = \dfrac{320}{1 + 0.2e^{-1.3x}}$? *(Lesson 8.8)*

    Ⓐ -1.24 Ⓑ 160
    Ⓒ 267 Ⓓ 320

18. **Short Response** You deposit $8500 into an account with 4% interest compounded daily. What is the balance after 1 year? after 10 years? after 18 years? *(Lesson 8.1)*

19. **Extended Response** A population of fish in a lake has been declining at an annual rate of 2%. The population of fish is currently estimated at 9000. *(Lessons 8.2, 8.6)*

    a. Write a model to find the number of fish f in the lake after t years.

    b. Evaluate the model for $t = 10$, 15, and 20 years.

    c. When will the population of fish be less than 2000?

Cumulative Practice *continued*
For use after Chapters 7–9

Chapter 9

Multiple Choice In Exercises 20–25, choose the letter of the correct answer.

20. In which table do x and y show direct variation? *(Lesson 9.1)*

    Ⓐ
x	0.5	1.0	1.5	2.0	2.5	3.0
y	1.2	2.1	3.0	3.9	4.8	5.7

    Ⓑ
x	0.5	1.0	1.5	2.0	2.5	3.0
y	16	8	$5\frac{1}{3}$	4	$3\frac{1}{5}$	$2\frac{2}{3}$

    Ⓒ
x	0.5	1.0	1.5	2.0	2.5	3.0
y	−4	1	−4	1	−4	1

    Ⓓ
x	0.5	1.0	1.5	2.0	2.5	3.0
y	0.15	0.30	0.45	0.6	0.75	0.9

21. What are the asymptotes of the graph of $y = \dfrac{3x}{4x - 3}$? *(Lesson 9.2)*

    Ⓐ $x = \frac{3}{4}, y = \frac{3}{4}$ Ⓑ $x = \frac{4}{3}, y = \frac{3}{4}$

    Ⓒ $x = \frac{3}{4}, y = 3$ Ⓓ $x = \frac{4}{3}, y = 3$

22. What are the x-intercepts of the graph of $y = \dfrac{x^3 - 8}{2x^2 + 11x - 6}$? *(Lesson 9.3)*

    Ⓐ −6 and 0.5
    Ⓑ 2
    Ⓒ −6, 0.5, and 2
    Ⓓ −6 and 2

23. What is a simplified form of $\dfrac{2x^2 + 3x}{2x^3 - x^2 - 6x}$? *(Lesson 9.4)*

    Ⓐ $\dfrac{2x + 3}{x - 2}$ Ⓑ $\dfrac{x}{x - 2}$

    Ⓒ $\dfrac{2x + 3}{x^2 - 2x}$ Ⓓ $\dfrac{1}{x - 2}$

24. What is a simplied form of $\dfrac{\frac{1}{2x}}{\frac{2}{x} - 1}$? *(Lesson 9.5)*

    Ⓐ $\dfrac{2 - x}{2x^2}$

    Ⓑ $\dfrac{1}{4 - 2x}$

    Ⓒ $\dfrac{2}{2 - x}$

    Ⓓ $\dfrac{1}{x - 2}$

25. What is the solution of $\dfrac{3}{x} - 2 = -\dfrac{7}{x}$? *(Lesson 9.6)*

    Ⓐ −8   Ⓑ −5
    Ⓒ 5   Ⓓ 8

26. **Short Response** In a relation, z varies jointly with w and y, and z varies inversely with x. If $w = 1$, $y = 1$, and $x = 1$, then $z = 4$. Write an equation for z in terms of w, y, and x. *(Lesson 9.1)*

27. **Extended Response** Use the equation $y = \dfrac{x^2 + x - 2}{x^2 - x - 2}$. *(Lesson 9.2)*

    a. Identify the x-intercepts. Explain.
    b. Identify the vertical asymptotes. Explain how you found them.
    c. Graph the function.

Chapter Standardized Test 10A

Multiple Choice

1. What is the midpoint of the segment joining $(-4, 7)$ and $(6, 3)$?
   - **A** $(1, 5)$
   - **B** $(5, 2)$
   - **C** $(1, 2)$
   - **D** $(5, 5)$

2. What is the standard form of the equation of the parabola with vertex at $(0, 0)$ and directrix $y = 4$?
   - **A** $x^2 = 16y$
   - **B** $x^2 = -16y$
   - **C** $x^2 = \frac{1}{16}y$
   - **D** $x^2 = -4y$

3. Which of the following is an equation of the line that is tangent to the circle $x^2 + y^2 = 18$ at $(3, -3)$?
   - **A** $y = -x + 6$
   - **B** $y = x + 6$
   - **C** $y = -x$
   - **D** $y = x - 6$

4. What are the foci of the ellipse with equation $4x^2 + 25y^2 = 100$?
   - **A** $(0, -\sqrt{29})$ and $(0, \sqrt{29})$
   - **B** $(-\sqrt{29}, 0)$ and $(\sqrt{29}, 0)$
   - **C** $(0, -\sqrt{21})$ and $(0, \sqrt{21})$
   - **D** $(-\sqrt{21}, 0)$ and $(\sqrt{21}, 0)$

5. What is an equation of the hyperbola with foci at $(-2, 0)$ and $(2, 0)$ and vertices at $\left(-\frac{1}{2}, 0\right)$ and $\left(\frac{1}{2}, 0\right)$?
   - **A** $4x^2 - \frac{4y^2}{15} = 1$
   - **B** $4y^2 - \frac{4x^2}{15} = 1$
   - **C** $\frac{x^2}{4} - \frac{y^2}{19} = 1$
   - **D** $\frac{y^2}{4} - \frac{x^2}{19} = 1$

6. What conic does the equation $9x^2 - 54x + 8y^2 - 16y + 17 = 0$ represent?
   - **A** parabola
   - **B** circle
   - **C** ellipse
   - **D** hyperbola

7. What are the points of intersection of the graphs of the system?
   $x^2 - 8y = 0$
   $2x^2 + 2y - 9x = 0$
   - **A** $(0, 0)$ and $(-4, 2)$
   - **B** $(0, 0)$ and $(-2, 4)$
   - **C** $(0, 0)$ and $(4, 2)$
   - **D** $(0, 0)$ and $(2, 4)$

Short Response

8. Find the distance between $(-4, 3)$ and $(5, 5)$.

Extended Response

9. Classify the conic section and write its equation in standard form. Then graph the equation.
   $x^2 + 2x + 9y^2 - 36y + 28 = 0$

Chapter Standardized Test 10B

Multiple Choice

1. What is the midpoint of the segment joining $(-5, 2)$ and $(3, -6)$?
   - Ⓐ $(4, -4)$
   - Ⓑ $(-1, -2)$
   - Ⓒ $(-1, -4)$
   - Ⓓ $(-2, 2)$

2. What is the standard form of the equation of the parabola with vertex at $(0, 0)$ and directrix $y = -3$?
   - Ⓐ $x^2 = 9y$
   - Ⓑ $x^2 = -9y$
   - Ⓒ $x^2 = -\frac{1}{9}y$
   - Ⓓ $x^2 = 3y$

3. Which of the following is an equation of the line that is tangent to the circle $x^2 + y^2 = 10$ at $(3, -1)$?
   - Ⓐ $y = -3x + 8$
   - Ⓑ $y = -\frac{1}{3}x$
   - Ⓒ $y = 3x - 10$
   - Ⓓ $y = \frac{1}{3}x - 2$

4. What are the foci of the ellipse with equation $x^2 + 2y^2 = 8$?
   - Ⓐ $(-2, 0)$ and $(2, 0)$
   - Ⓑ $(-\sqrt{12}, 0)$ and $(\sqrt{12}, 0)$
   - Ⓒ $(0, -2)$ and $(0, 2)$
   - Ⓓ $(0, -\sqrt{12})$ and $(0, \sqrt{12})$

5. What is an equation of the hyperbola with foci at $(-5, 0)$ and $(5, 0)$ and vertices at $(-1, 0)$ and $(1, 0)$?
   - Ⓐ $\frac{x^2}{24} - \frac{y^2}{1} = 1$
   - Ⓑ $\frac{y^2}{24} - \frac{x^2}{1} = 1$
   - Ⓒ $\frac{y^2}{1} - \frac{x^2}{24} = 1$
   - Ⓓ $\frac{x^2}{1} - \frac{y^2}{24} = 1$

6. What conic does the equation $-4x^2 + 3y^2 + 6y - 9 = 0$ represent?
   - Ⓐ parabola
   - Ⓑ circle
   - Ⓒ ellipse
   - Ⓓ hyperbola

7. What are the points of intersection of the graphs of the system?
   $y^2 - 2x + 2 = 0$
   $x^2 + y^2 - 2x - 4y + 1 = 0$
   - Ⓐ $(1, 2)$ and $(2, 3)$
   - Ⓑ $(1, 2)$ and $(3, 2)$
   - Ⓒ $(1, 0)$ and $(3, 2)$
   - Ⓓ $(1, 0)$ and $(2, 3)$

Short Response

8. Find the distance between $(-7, -6)$ and $(-2, 5)$.

Extended Response

9. Classify the conic section and write its equation in standard form. Then graph the equation.
   $x^2 + y^2 - 4x + 4y - 1 = 0$

Chapter Standardized Test 11A

Multiple Choice

1. What is a rule for the nth term in the sequence $\frac{1}{2}, -2, 8, -32, \ldots$?

   Ⓐ $a_n = \frac{1}{2}(-4)^n$

   Ⓑ $a_n = -\frac{1}{8}(-4)^n$

   Ⓒ $a_n = \frac{1}{8}(-4)^n$

   Ⓓ $a_n = -\frac{1}{2}(-4)^n$

2. What is the sum of the first 25 terms of the series $3 + 9 + 15 + 21 + 27 + \cdots$?

   Ⓐ 1050   Ⓑ 1580

   Ⓒ 1875   Ⓓ 3675

3. What is the tenth term in the sequence $200, 40, 8, 1.6, 0.32, \ldots$?

   Ⓐ 0.0001024

   Ⓑ 0.000512

   Ⓒ 0.002048

   Ⓓ 0.00256

4. Which infinite geometric series does *not* have a sum?

   Ⓐ $\sum_{n=1}^{\infty} 5\left(\frac{1}{4}\right)^n$

   Ⓑ $\sum_{n=1}^{\infty} 1\left(-\frac{3}{4}\right)^n$

   Ⓒ $\sum_{n=1}^{\infty} \frac{2}{3}\left(\frac{8}{7}\right)^n$

   Ⓓ $\sum_{n=1}^{\infty} \frac{1}{3}\left(\frac{9}{10}\right)^n$

5. What is a recursive rule for the sequence $15, 19, 23, 28, 33, \ldots$?

   Ⓐ $a_1 = 15, a_n = 5a_{n-1}$

   Ⓑ $a_1 = 15, a_n = a_{n-1} + 5$

   Ⓒ $a_1 = 15, a_n = a_{n-1} + 15$

   Ⓓ $a_1 = 15, a_n = 15a_{n-1}$

6. The sequence below shows a square in which one third of the remaining white part is shaded with each iteration. What fraction of the eighth square would be white?

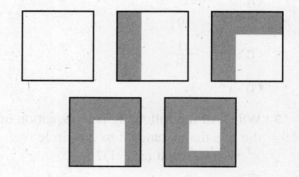

   Ⓐ $\frac{1}{2187}$ Ⓑ $\frac{2}{3}$

   Ⓒ $\frac{128}{2187}$ Ⓓ $\frac{256}{6561}$

Short Response

7. Write a recursive rule for the sequence $100, 98, 94, 86, 70, \ldots$.

Extended Response

8. Write the next 5 terms of the sequence. Then write a rule for the nth term.

   $8, 12, 16, 20, 24, \ldots$

Chapter Standardized Test 11B

Multiple Choice

1. What is a rule for the nth term in the sequence $\frac{1}{9}, \frac{2}{3}, 4, 24, \ldots$?

   A $a_n = \frac{1}{54}(6)^n$

   B $a_n = \frac{1}{9}(6)^n$

   C $a_n = 6\left(\frac{2}{3}\right)^n$

   D $a_n = \frac{1}{9}\left(\frac{2}{3}\right)^n$

2. What is the sum of the first 18 terms of the series $125 + 121 + 117 + 113 + \cdots$?

   A 1496 **B** 1602
   C 1638 **D** 1690

3. What is the seventeenth term in the sequence $\frac{3}{16}, \frac{3}{8}, \frac{3}{4}, 1\frac{1}{2}, \ldots$?

   A 4096 **B** 8192
   C 10,668 **D** 12,288

4. Which infinite geometric series does *not* have a sum?

   A $\sum_{n=1}^{\infty} 5\left(\frac{6}{5}\right)^n$

   B $\sum_{n=1}^{\infty} 8\left(-\frac{1}{4}\right)^n$

   C $\sum_{n=1}^{\infty} \frac{2}{3}\left(-\frac{3}{7}\right)^n$

   D $\sum_{n=1}^{\infty} \frac{1}{3}\left(\frac{3}{4}\right)^n$

5. What is a recursive rule for the sequence $135, 90, 60, 40, \ldots$?

   A $a_1 = 135, a_n = \frac{3}{10}a_{n-1}$

   B $a_1 = 135, a_n = \frac{3}{2}a_{n-1}$

   C $a_1 = 135, a_n = \frac{2}{3}a_{n-1}$

   D $a_1 = 135, a_n = \frac{1}{3}a_{n-1}$

6. The sequence below shows a triangle in which one half of the remaining white part is shaded with each iteration. What fraction of the 7th triangle would be shaded?

   A $\frac{1}{128}$ **B** $\frac{63}{64}$

   C $\frac{127}{128}$ **D** $\frac{33}{64}$

Short Response

7. Write a recursive rule for the sequence $5, 6, 9, 14, 21, \ldots$.

Extended Response

8. Write the next 5 terms in the sequence. Then write a rule for the nth term.

   $80, 75, 70, 65, 60, \ldots$

Chapter Standardized Test 12A

Multiple Choice

1. A lock code is 3 digits long. Each digit can be one of the numbers from 1 to 5. How many lock combinations are possible?

   (A) 15   (B) 60   (C) 125   (D) 243

2. How many ways can you choose 4 students from a class of 24?

   (A) 276   (B) 552
   (C) 5313   (D) 10,626

3. You are to draw a card at random from a deck of 52 cards. What is the probability that you draw one of the 4 aces?

   (A) $\frac{1}{13}$ (B) $\frac{1}{12}$ (C) $\frac{1}{4}$ (D) $\frac{1}{3}$

4. An integer from 1 to 20 is selected at random. What is the probability that it is divisible by 3 or even?

   (A) $\frac{3}{20}$ (B) $\frac{3}{10}$ (C) $\frac{7}{20}$ (D) $\frac{13}{20}$

5. The probability that it will rain is 0.7. The probability that you will miss your bus is 0.1. What is the probability that it rains and you catch your bus?

   (A) 0.03   (B) 0.07
   (C) 0.27   (D) 0.63

6. What is the probability that you get exactly 9 heads in 15 coin tosses?

   (A) about 0.153   (B) about 0.161
   (C) about 0.184   (D) about 0.226

7. A normal distribution such as the one shown below has a mean of 18 and a standard deviation of 3. About what percent of the data falls between 9 and 15?

   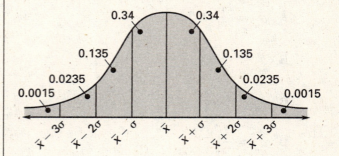

   (A) 14%   (B) 16%
   (C) 48%   (D) 50%

Short Response

8. The Venn diagram below shows the number of students in math class who participate in school music (A) and school sports (B). If all students participate in music, sports, or both, what is the probability that a student selected at random participates in both music and sports?

   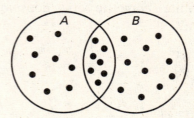

Extended Response

9. Define the complement of an event. Give an example.

Chapter Standardized Test 12B

Multiple Choice

1. A lock code is 6 digits long. Each digit can be one of the numbers from 1 to 4. How many lock combinations are possible?

    Ⓐ 24   Ⓑ 144   Ⓒ 1296   Ⓓ 4096

2. How many ways can you choose 7 students from a class of 26?

    Ⓐ 249,964   Ⓑ 6,249,100
    Ⓒ 657,800   Ⓓ 24,996,400

3. You are to draw a card at random from a deck of 52 cards. What is the probability that you draw one of the 8 kings and queens?

    Ⓐ $\frac{1}{13}$ Ⓑ $\frac{2}{13}$ Ⓒ $\frac{2}{11}$ Ⓓ $\frac{1}{4}$

4. An integer from 1 to 10 is selected at random. What is the probability that it is divisible by 3 or odd?

    Ⓐ $\frac{7}{10}$ Ⓑ $\frac{3}{5}$ Ⓒ $\frac{3}{10}$ Ⓓ $\frac{1}{10}$

5. The probability that it will rain is 0.6. The probability that you will miss your bus is 0.2. What is the probability that it rains and you catch your bus?

    Ⓐ 0.12   Ⓑ 0.32   Ⓒ 0.48   Ⓓ 0.8

6. What is the probability that you get exactly 7 heads in 12 coin tosses?

    Ⓐ about 0.142   Ⓑ about 0.193
    Ⓒ about 0.226   Ⓓ about 0.408

7. A normal distribution such as the one shown below has a mean of 22 and a standard deviation of 3. About what percent of the data falls between 16 and 25?

    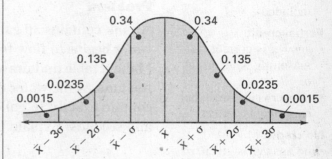

    Ⓐ 48%   Ⓑ 68%
    Ⓒ 82%   Ⓓ 95%

Short Response

8. The Venn diagram below shows the people who can use two different computer programs A and B in an office. What is the probability that an employee selected at random can use program A?

    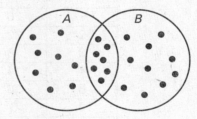

Extended Response

9. Define *mutually exclusive events*. Give an example.

Building Test-Taking Skills

For use after Chapters 10–12

Scoring Rubric

Full credit
- answer is correct, *and*
- work or reasoning is included

Partial credit
- answer is correct, but reasoning is incorrect, *or*
- answer is incorrect, but reasoning is correct

No credit
- no answer is given, *or*
- answer makes no sense

Strategies for Answering
Extended Response Questions

Problem

A tank contains 30 gallons of water. You pull out the drain plug, and water begins to flow from the tank at a rate of 4 gallons per minute. Make a table and draw a graph that shows the amount of water in the tank as the water drains. After how much time will the tank contain exactly 16 gallons of water? Give your answer in minutes and seconds. Explain how you found your answer.

Full credit solution

In the graph, the horizontal axis shows minutes after pulling the plug, and the vertical axis shows the gallons of water in the tank.

The table and graph are correct and reflect an understanding of the problem.

minutes	gallons
0	30
1	26
2	22
3	18
4	14
5	10
6	6
7	2

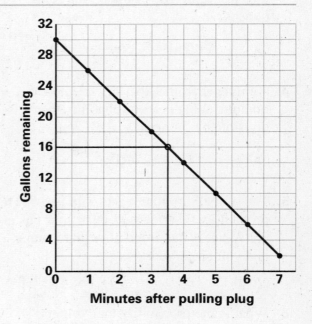

The answer is correct. — After 3 minutes and 30 seconds, the tank will contain 16 gallons of water.

The reasoning behind the answer is explained clearly. — To find my answer, I looked at the graph and saw that the tank will hold 16 gallons at $3\frac{1}{2}$ minutes. Because $\frac{1}{2}$ of a minute equals 30 seconds, I know that the tank will hold 16 gallons of water after 3 minutes and 30 seconds.

Building Test-Taking Skills *continued*

For use after Chapters 10–12

Partial credit solution

The table and graph are correct.

minutes	0	1	2	3	4
gallons	30	26	22	18	14

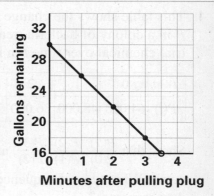

The answer is incorrect. — The tank will hold 16 gallons after 3 minutes and 5 seconds.
The graph shows that there are 16 gallons after 3.5 minutes.

No credit solution

The table is correct, but there is no graph.

minutes	0	1	2	3	4
gallons	30	26	22	18	14

The answer is incorrect, and there is no explanation. — The tank will never have exactly 16 gallons in it.

Watch Out! Scoring is often based on how clearly you explain your reasoning.

Your turn now

1. Score one student's answer to the problem on the previous page as *full credit, partial credit,* or *no credit.* Explain your choice. If you choose *partial credit* or *no credit,* explain how to change the answer so that it earns *full credit.*

minutes	0	1	2	3	4
gallons	30	26	22	18	14

The tank will have 16 gallons after 3 minutes and 30 seconds. The table shows that the tank will have 16 gallons between 3 and 4 minutes. 16 is halfway between 14 and 18. So, the tank must have 16 gallons halfway between 3 and 4 minutes. The tank has 16 gallons at 3 minutes and 30 seconds.

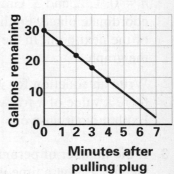

Name _____ Date _____

Practicing Test-Taking Skills
For use after Chapters 10–12

Extended Response

1. This table shows the change in population P in a colony of bacteria treated with a trial chemical over time t in hours.

t	0	1	2	3	4
$P(t)$	64,000	48,000	36,000	27,000	20,250

   Show that $\frac{P(1)}{P(0)}, \frac{P(2)}{P(1)}, \frac{P(3)}{P(2)},$ and $\frac{P(4)}{P(3)}$ are equal. What type of sequence does the data represent?

   Model this data using an exponential function. Identify the function as exponential growth or exponential decay. Interpret the numbers in the equation.

   Estimate the population after 8 hours. Estimate the number of hours it will take for the population to fall below 1000.

2. Let n represent a counting number. The equations $x = n - 3$ and $y = n^2 + 1$ determine a point in the plane for each value of n.

   Make a table of values for (x, y) using $n = 0, 1, 2,$ and 3. Graph the points in a coordinate plane. Predict the coordinates of the next point in the sequence from the graph.

   Write an equation for y in terms of x. Is there a value of x for which $y = 100$? Explain your answer.

3. If the number of permutations of n objects taken $n - 2$ at a time is 60, how many objects are in the set? If three of the objects are the same, how many distinguishable permutations can be made?

4. Write a radical equation using the Pythagorean theorem to find x. What are the lengths of $\overline{AB}$ and $\overline{AC}$?

   Give your answer to the nearest tenth. Show your work.

   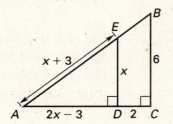

5. Your newspaper deliverer throws the paper so that it lands somewhere on your porch, which is 12 feet long. What is the probability that it will land in front of your 3-foot-wide door? Explain your response.

6. Find the intersection points of these equations:

   $x^2 + y^2 = 25$

   $x - y = 5$

   Make a graph of the two equations to verify your answer. What would the intersection points be if the radius of the circle was doubled?

Cumulative Practice

For use after Chapters 10–12

Chapter 10

Multiple Choice In Exercises 1–7, choose the letter of the correct answer.

1. What is an equation for the perpendicular bisector of the line segment joining $(3, 7)$ and $(-1, -1)$? *(Lesson 10.1)*

    Ⓐ $y = 2x + 1$
    Ⓑ $y = -\frac{1}{2}x + 3\frac{1}{2}$
    Ⓒ $y = \frac{1}{2}x + 2\frac{1}{2}$
    Ⓓ $y = -2x + 5$

2. What is an equation of the parabola with vertex at $(0, 0)$ and directrix $x = 2\frac{1}{2}$? *(Lesson 10.2)*

    Ⓐ $x^2 = 10x$ Ⓑ $x^2 = -10x$
    Ⓒ $y^2 = 10x$ Ⓓ $y^2 = -10x$

3. What is an equation of the circle that passes through $(2, -6)$ and whose center is the origin? *(Lesson 10.3)*

    Ⓐ $x^2 + y^2 = 40$
    Ⓑ $x^2 + y^2 = 2\sqrt{10}$
    Ⓒ $2x^2 + 6y^2 = 1$
    Ⓓ $6x^2 + 2y^2 = 40$

4. What is an equation for an ellipse with vertices $(-6, 0)$ and $(6, 0)$ and co-vertices $(0, 3)$ and $(0, -3)$? *(Lesson 10.4)*

    Ⓐ $\frac{x^2}{9} + \frac{y^2}{36} = 1$
    Ⓑ $\frac{x^2}{36} + \frac{y^2}{9} = 1$
    Ⓒ $\frac{x^2}{36} - \frac{y^2}{9} = 1$
    Ⓓ $\frac{x^2}{6} + \frac{y^2}{3} = 1$

5. What are the asymptotes of the graph of the hyperbola described by the equation $\frac{x^2}{9} - \frac{y^2}{25} = 1$? *(Lesson 10.5)*

    Ⓐ $y = \frac{3}{5}x, y = -\frac{5}{3}x$
    Ⓑ $y = \frac{5}{3}x, y = -\frac{3}{5}x$
    Ⓒ $y = \frac{3}{5}x, y = -\frac{3}{5}x$
    Ⓓ $y = \frac{5}{3}x, y = -\frac{5}{3}x$

6. What is the center of the hyperbola described by the equation $x^2 - 9y^2 - 4x - 36y - 41 = 0$? *(Lesson 10.6)*

    Ⓐ $(2, 18)$ Ⓑ $(-2, -18)$
    Ⓒ $(2, -2)$ Ⓓ $(-2, 2)$

7. What are the points of intersection of the graphs in the system? *(Lesson 10.7)*

    $x^2 + y^2 + 2x + 2y = 8$
    $x - y = 4$

    Ⓐ $(4, 0)$ and $(0, 2)$
    Ⓑ $(4, 0)$ and $(2, -2)$
    Ⓒ $(0, -4)$ and $(2, -2)$
    Ⓓ $(0, -4)$ and $(-4, 0)$

8. **Short Response** What is the midpoint of the segment joining $(-3.6, -2.8)$ and $(12.4, 9.2)$? *(Lesson 10.1)*

9. **Extended Response** Identify the vertices, co-vertices, and foci of the ellipse $\frac{x^2}{16} + \frac{y^2}{9} = 1$. *(Lesson 10.4)*

Cumulative Practice continued
For use after Chapters 10–12

Chapter 11

Multiple Choice In Exercises 10–16, choose the letter of the correct answer.

10. What is a rule for the nth term of the sequence shown in the graph? *(Lesson 11.1)*

    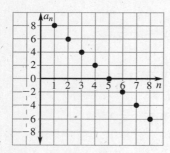

    Ⓐ $a_n = 8 - 2n$
    Ⓑ $a_n = 10 - 2n$
    Ⓒ $a_n = 2n - 8$
    Ⓓ $a_n = 2n - 10$

11. What is the sum of the first 20 terms of the series? *(Lesson 11.2)*

    $9 + 13 + 17 + 21 + 25 + \cdots$

    Ⓐ 940
    Ⓑ 980
    Ⓒ 1880
    Ⓓ 1960

12. What is a_{37} in the sequence below? *(Lesson 11.2)*

    150, 148, 146, 144, 142, . . .

    Ⓐ 76
    Ⓑ 78
    Ⓒ 94
    Ⓓ 113

13. Two terms of a geometric sequence are $a_3 = 4$ and $a_6 = 256$. What is a rule for the nth term? *(Lesson 11.3)*

    Ⓐ $a_n = 4(2)^n$
    Ⓑ $a_n = (4)^{n-1}$
    Ⓒ $a_n = \frac{1}{4}(4)^n$
    Ⓓ $a_n = \frac{1}{4}(4)^{n-1}$

14. What is the sum of the first 13 terms of the geometric series? *(Lesson 11.3)*

    $1 + 3 + 9 + 27 + 81 + \cdots$

    Ⓐ 345,437
    Ⓑ 531,441
    Ⓒ 797,161
    Ⓓ 1,594,323

15. What is the sum of the infinite geometric series? *(Lesson 11.4)*

    $$\sum_{n=1}^{\infty} 15(0.8)^{n-1}$$

    Ⓐ 15.8
    Ⓑ 18.75
    Ⓒ 75
    Ⓓ 120

16. What are the first five terms of the sequence? *(Lesson 11.5)*

    $a_0 = 8$
    $a_n = a_{n-1} + 2(n-1)$

    Ⓐ 8, 10, 14, 20, 28
    Ⓑ 8, 8, 10, 14, 20
    Ⓒ 8, 12, 16, 22, 30
    Ⓓ 8, 12, 18, 24, 32

17. **Short Response** Write the first five terms of the sequence. *(Lesson 11.5)*

    $a_0 = 5$
    $a_n = a_{n-1} + (-1)^n$

18. **Extended Response** A sequence is defined by $a_n = 18 + 3n$. *(Lesson 11.1)*

    a. Write the first six terms of the sequence.

    b. Find the forty-third term of the sequence.

Cumulative Practice *continued*
For use after Chapters 10–12

Chapter 12
Multiple Choice Exercises 19–25, choose the letter of the correct answer.

19. How many distinguishable permutations of the letters in SOCCER are possible? *(Lesson 12.1)*

    (A) 360   (B) 480   (C) 600   (D) 720

20. What is the expansion of $(2x + 3)^4$? *(Lesson 12.2)*

    (A) $16x^4 + 144x^3 + 216x^2 + 144x + 81$
    (B) $16x^4 + 96x^3 + 216x^2 + 216x + 81$
    (C) $16x^4 + 96x^3 + 288x^2 + 216x + 81$
    (D) $16x^4 + 144x^3 + 288x^2 + 144x + 81$

21. A poll asked 80 twelfth grade students what grade they would like to tutor. The results are shown below.

    12 students prefer K–3.
    34 students prefer 4–5.
    7 students prefer 6–8.
    12 students prefer 9–11.
    15 students prefer grade 12.

    What is the probability that a randomly selected twelfth grader would choose to tutor grades K–3 or 4–5? *(Lesson 12.3)*

    (A) 0.15   (B) 0.425
    (C) 0.46   (D) 0.575

22. A number from 1 to 100 is selected at random. What expression can you use to find the probability that it is divisible by 5 or by 2? *(Lesson 12.4)*

    (A) $0.2 + 0.5 - 0.1$
    (B) $0.2 + 0.5$
    (C) $0.1 + 0.5$
    (D) $0.1 + 0.5 - 0.2$

23. A and B are dependent events. $P(A) = 0.55$ and $P(B \mid A) = 0.40$. What is $P(A \text{ and } B)$? *(Lesson 12.5)*

    (A) 0.15   (B) 0.22   (C) 0.40   (D) 0.95

24. A poll finds that 43% of the adults surveyed support the president. If 8 adults are surveyed, what is the probability that exactly 4 of them support the president? *(Lesson 12.6)*

    (A) 0.027   (B) 0.080
    (C) 0.253   (D) 0.78

25. The mean score on an exam was 79, with a standard deviation of 5.5. About what percentage of students scored between 67 and 79? *(Lesson 12.7)*

    (A) 31%   (B) 48%   (C) 65%   (D) 87%

26. **Short Response** There is a 3% chance that you have a medical condition. A preliminary test is 95% accurate for people who have the condition and 90% accurate for people who do not have the condition. What is the probability that you have the condition and the test detects it? *(Lesson 12.5)*

27. **Extended Response** A subway commuter experiences a delay of 10 minutes or more on 3 days out of 20. She works on the train 4 days out of 5. *(Lessons 12.3, 12.4)*

    a. What is the probability that she is not delayed?

    b. What is the probability that she is delayed and works on the train?

    c. What is the probability that she is not delayed and does not work on the train?

Chapter Standardized Test 13A

Multiple Choice

1. What is the value of *x* in the triangle shown?

   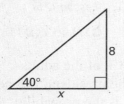

   - (A) 5.14
   - (B) 6.71
   - (C) 9.53
   - (D) 12.44

2. What is the arc length of a sector with radius 8 centimeters and central angle 135°?

   - (A) 2.4 cm
   - (B) 12.6 cm
   - (C) 15.4 cm
   - (D) 18.8 cm

3. What is the value of sin −90°?

   - (A) −1
   - (B) −0.5
   - (C) 0
   - (D) 1

4. What is the value of *x* in the triangle below?

   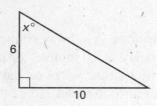

   - (A) 31.0
   - (B) 36.9
   - (C) 53.1
   - (D) 59.0

5. What is the area of the triangle?

   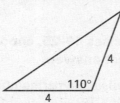

   - (A) 1.88
   - (B) 2.73
   - (C) 7.52
   - (D) 9.31

6. What is the value of *x* in the triangle below?

   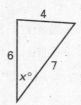

   - (A) 28.4
   - (B) 34.8
   - (C) 69.8
   - (D) 88.0

7. In the parametric equations, what are the values for *x* and *y* at $t = 14$?

   $x = -t + 3$
   $y = -2t$

   - (A) (−11, −28)
   - (B) (−11, −146)
   - (C) (17, −28)
   - (D) (17, −140)

Short Response

8. Write an *xy*-equation for the parametric equations and state the domain:

   $x = -3t + 1$ and $y = 4t$ for $0 \leq t \leq 8$

Extended Response

9. Solve the triangle.

Chapter Standardized Test 13B

Multiple Choice

1. What is the value of x in the triangle shown?

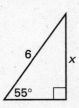

  A 3.44
  B 4.91
  C 7.66
  D 8.57

2. What is the arc length of a sector with radius 5 centimeters and central angle 60°?

  A 2.6 cm
  B 3.9 cm
  C 5.2 cm
  D 7.3 cm

3. What is the value of $\cos -90°$?

  A -1 **B** -0.5
  C 0 **D** 1

4. What is the value of x in the triangle below?

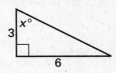

  A 26.6   **B** 30.0
  C 42.8   **D** 63.4

5. What is the area of the triangle?

  A 1.27   **B** 7.61
  C 9.41   **D** 15.21

6. What is the value of x in the triangle shown?

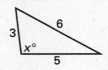

  A 93.8   **B** 102.1
  C 109.7   **D** 113.8

7. In the parametric equations, what are the values for x and y at $t = 12$?

  $x = -t + 7$
  $y = -2t + 4$

  A $(-5, 14)$ **B** $(-5, -20)$
  C $(-19, 42)$ **D** $(-19, -24)$

Short Response

8. Write an xy-equation for the parametric equations and state the domain:

  $x = \frac{1}{2}t + 3$ and $y = -2t$ for $0 \le t \le 8$

Extended Response

9. Solve the triangle.

Chapter Standardized Test 14A

Multiple Choice

1. What is the period of the function $y = 3 \cos \frac{\pi x}{2}$?

   Ⓐ 1
   Ⓑ $\frac{\pi}{2}$
   Ⓒ 4
   Ⓓ 4π

2. Which function matches the graph shown below?

   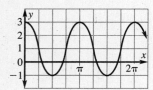

   Ⓐ $y = 1 + 2 \cos 2x$
   Ⓑ $y = 1 + 2 \sin 2x$
   Ⓒ $y = 1 + 2 \sin \frac{x}{2}$
   Ⓓ $y = 1 + 2 \cos \frac{x}{2}$

3. What is the simplified form of the expression $\cos x \sec x - \tan^2 x \cos^2 x$?

   Ⓐ $\csc^2 x$ Ⓑ $\cos^2 x$
   Ⓒ $1 - \sec^2 x$ Ⓓ $1 - \sin x \cos x$

4. What is the solution of $4 \sin^2 x \cos x = -\cos x$ on the interval $0 \leq x \leq \pi$?

   Ⓐ $\frac{\pi}{4}$ Ⓑ $\frac{3\pi}{8}$
   Ⓒ $\frac{\pi}{2}$ Ⓓ $\frac{3\pi}{4}$

5. Which function has a minimum at $(\pi, 1)$ and a maximum at $(\frac{\pi}{3}, 8)$?

   Ⓐ $f(x) = 4.5 + 3.5 \sin 3x$
   Ⓑ $f(x) = 1 + 7 \sin \frac{3x}{2}$
   Ⓒ $f(x) = 4.5 + 3.5 \sin \frac{3x}{2}$
   Ⓓ $f(x) = 1 + 7 \sin 3x$

6. What is the exact value of $\sin \frac{5\pi}{12}$?

   Ⓐ $\frac{\sqrt{6}}{4}$ Ⓑ $\frac{\sqrt{6} + \sqrt{2}}{4}$
   Ⓒ $\frac{\sqrt{2}}{4}$ Ⓓ $\frac{\sqrt{6} - \sqrt{2}}{4}$

7. What is the solution of the equation $2 \sin \frac{x}{2} - \cos x = \frac{1}{2}$ for $0 \leq x \leq \pi$?

   Ⓐ $\frac{\pi}{6}$ Ⓑ $\frac{\pi}{4}$
   Ⓒ $\frac{\pi}{3}$ Ⓓ π

Short Response

8. Given that $\cos x = -\frac{1}{4}$ and $90° \leq x \leq 180°$, what are the values of the other five trigonometric functions of x?

Extended Response

9. Write a function for the sinusoid.

   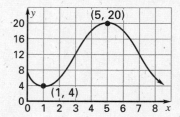

Chapter Standardized Test 14B

Multiple Choice

1. What is the period of the function $y = \frac{3}{4}\cos 3\pi x$?

   Ⓐ $\frac{2}{3}$ Ⓑ $\frac{\pi}{2}$

   Ⓒ 3 Ⓓ 4

2. Which function matches the graph shown below?

   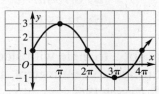

   Ⓐ $y = 1 + 2\cos 2x$

   Ⓑ $y = 1 + 2\sin 2x$

   Ⓒ $y = 1 + 2\sin \frac{x}{2}$

   Ⓓ $y = 1 + 2\cos \frac{x}{2}$

3. What is a simplified form of the expression $\cos x \sec x + \cot^2 x \sin^3 x \sec^3 x$?

   Ⓐ $\sec^2 x$ Ⓑ $\csc^2 x$

   Ⓒ $1 + \tan x$ Ⓓ $1 + \sin x \cos x$

4. What is the solution of $3\tan^2 x = 1$ on the interval $0 \leq x \leq \pi$?

   Ⓐ $\frac{\pi}{6}$ Ⓑ $\frac{\pi}{6}$ or $\frac{5\pi}{6}$

   Ⓒ $\frac{\pi}{6}$ or $\frac{2\pi}{3}$ Ⓓ $\frac{2\pi}{3}$ or $\frac{5\pi}{6}$

5. Which function has a maximum at $(0, 2)$ and a minimum at $\left(\frac{\pi}{2}, 0\right)$?

   Ⓐ $f(x) = 1 + 2\cos 2x$

   Ⓑ $f(x) = 1 + 2\cos \frac{x}{2}$

   Ⓒ $f(x) = 1 + \cos \frac{x}{2}$

   Ⓓ $f(x) = 1 + \cos 2x$

6. What is the exact value of $\cos \frac{5\pi}{12}$?

   Ⓐ $\frac{\sqrt{6}}{4}$ Ⓑ $\frac{\sqrt{6} + \sqrt{2}}{4}$

   Ⓒ $\frac{\sqrt{2}}{4}$ Ⓓ $\frac{\sqrt{6} - \sqrt{2}}{4}$

7. What is the solution of the equation $\tan \frac{x}{2} - \sin x = 0$ for $0 \leq x \leq \pi$?

   Ⓐ $\frac{\pi}{4}$ Ⓑ $\frac{\pi}{3}$

   Ⓒ $\frac{\pi}{2}$ Ⓓ $\frac{3\pi}{4}$

Short Response

8. Given that $\cos x = -\frac{1}{3}$ and $90° \leq x \leq 180°$, what are the values of the other five trigonometric functions of x?

Extended Response

9. Write a function for the sinusoid.

Cumulative Practice

For use after Chapters 13–14

Chapter 13

Multiple Choice In Exercises 1–7, choose the letter of the correct answer.

1. What is the solution? *(Lesson 13.1)*

   $\tan 60° = \dfrac{8}{x}$

   Ⓐ $8\sqrt{3}$ Ⓑ $\dfrac{\sqrt{3}}{16}$ Ⓒ $\dfrac{\sqrt{3}}{8}$ Ⓓ $\dfrac{8\sqrt{3}}{3}$

2. Which pair of angles are coterminal? *(Lesson 13.2)*

   Ⓐ $-100°$ and $620°$
   Ⓑ $-330°$ and $570°$
   Ⓒ $-180°$ and $720°$
   Ⓓ $-120°$ and $480°$

3. Let $(-7, 3)$ be a point on the terminal side of an angle θ in standard position. What is the value of $\cos\theta$? *(Lesson 13.3)*

   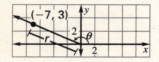

   Ⓐ $-\dfrac{7\sqrt{58}}{58}$ Ⓑ $-\dfrac{3\sqrt{58}}{58}$
   Ⓒ $\dfrac{3\sqrt{58}}{58}$ Ⓓ $\dfrac{7\sqrt{58}}{58}$

4. Given that $0 \le \theta \le \pi$, what is the value of θ in radians? *(Lesson 13.4)*

   $\tan\theta = -\dfrac{5}{3}$

   Ⓐ 1.030 radians   Ⓑ 2.112 radians
   Ⓒ 2.863 radians   Ⓓ 3.011 radians

5. What is the area of the triangle? *(Lesson 13.5)*

   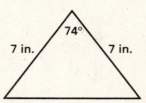

   Ⓐ 3.36 in.²   Ⓑ 6.73 in.²
   Ⓒ 18.44 in.²   Ⓓ 23.55 in.²

6. What is the area of a triangle with side lengths 4 centimeters, 6 centimeters, and 8 centimeters? *(Lesson 13.6)*

   Ⓐ 3.87 cm²   Ⓑ 11.62 cm²
   Ⓒ 12.25 cm²   Ⓓ 16.43 cm²

7. What is an xy-equation for the parametric equations $x = -3t$ and $y = 2t + 1$? *(Lesson 13.7)*

   Ⓐ $y = -\dfrac{1}{6}x - \dfrac{1}{2}$ Ⓑ $y = -\dfrac{3}{2}x + \dfrac{1}{2}$
   Ⓒ $y = -\dfrac{2}{3}x + 1$ Ⓓ $y = -6x + 1$

8. **Short Response** What is the area of a sector of a circle with radius 8 feet and central angle 22°? *(Lesson 13.2)*

9. **Extended Response** A shot put is hurled with an initial velocity of 98 ft/sec at an angle of 35° from a position 5 ft above the ground, corresponding to (0, 5). Write parametric equations for x and y. (Use $g = 32$ ft/sec².) Find (x, y) after 3 seconds. *(Lesson 13.7)*

Cumulative Practice *continued*

For use after Chapters 13–14

Chapter 14

Multiple Choice In Exercises 10–16, choose the letter of the correct answer.

10. What is the range of the function $y = -2 \cos 3x + 4$? *(Lesson 14.1)*

    A $0 \leq y \leq 4$ **B** $0 \leq y \leq 6$
    C $1 \leq y \leq 5$ **D** $2 \leq y \leq 6$

11. What are the asymptotes in the graph of $y = \frac{1}{2} \tan 2\left(x - \frac{\pi}{4}\right)$ in the interval $0 \leq x \leq 2\pi$? *(Lesson 14.2)*

    A $x = 0, x = \frac{\pi}{2}, x = \pi, x = \frac{3\pi}{2},$ and $x = 2\pi$
    B $x = \frac{\pi}{4}, x = \frac{3\pi}{4},$ and $x = \frac{5\pi}{4}$
    C $x = \frac{3\pi}{4}$ and $x = \frac{7\pi}{4}$
    D $x = \frac{\pi}{4}$ and $x = \frac{3\pi}{4}$

12. What is a simplified form of the expression $\tan\left(\frac{\pi}{2} - \theta\right) \sin \theta$? *(Lesson 14.3)*

    A $-\sin^2 \theta$ **B** $\cos \theta$
    C $\sin \theta \cos \theta$ **D** $-\sin \theta \cos \theta$

13. What is the general solution of the equation $\cos x (2 \sin x - 1) = 2 - 4 \sin x$? Assume n is an integer. *(Lesson 14.4)*

    A $x = \frac{\pi}{6} + 2n\pi$ or $x = \frac{11\pi}{6} + 2n\pi$
    B $x = \frac{\pi}{6} + 2n\pi$ or $x = \frac{5\pi}{6} + 2n\pi$
    C $x = \frac{\pi}{3} + 2n\pi$ or $x = \frac{5\pi}{3} + 2n\pi$
    D $x = \frac{\pi}{3} + 2n\pi$ or $x = \frac{2\pi}{3} + 2n\pi$

14. Which function matches the sinusoid? *(Lesson 14.5)*

    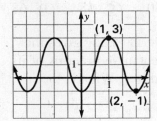

    A $y = 2 \cos \pi x - 1$
    B $y = -\cos \pi x + 2$
    C $y = \cos \pi x - 2$
    D $y = -2 \cos \pi x + 1$

15. What is a simplified form of the expression $\tan\left(\frac{\pi}{4} - x\right)$? *(Lesson 14.6)*

    A $-\tan x$ **B** $1 - \tan x$
    C $\frac{1 - \tan x}{1 + \tan x}$ **D** $\frac{1 + \tan x}{1 - \tan x}$

16. What is a simplified form of the expression $\frac{\cos 2\theta}{\cos \theta}$? *(Lesson 14.7)*

    A $2 \cos^2 \theta - \sec \theta$
    B $2 \sin \theta$
    C $2 \cos \theta - \sec \theta$
    D $\cos \theta + 2 \sec \theta$

17. **Short Response** Graph one cycle of $y = \sin 2x$. *(Lesson 14.1)*

18. **Extended Response** Verify the identity $(\sin^2 x)(1 + \sec^2 x) = \sec^2 x - \cos^2 x$. *(Lesson 14.3)*

Post-Course Test

1. What is the value of the expression $2x^2 + x - 3y + 4$ for $x = -5$ and $y = -3$?

   Ⓐ -42 Ⓑ 50 Ⓒ 58 Ⓓ 68

2. The formula $P = 2\ell + 2w$ gives the perimeter of a rectangle in terms of its length ℓ and width w. What is the equation for w?

   Ⓐ $w = \frac{1}{2}(P - 2\ell)$ Ⓑ $w = \frac{1}{2}(P - \ell)$

   Ⓒ $w = 2P - \ell$ Ⓓ $w = \frac{1}{2}(P + 2\ell)$

3. What is the solution of the equality $\left|\frac{2}{3}x + 4\right| = 9$?

   Ⓐ $-7\frac{1}{2}$ or $7\frac{1}{2}$

   Ⓑ $-19\frac{1}{2}$ or $7\frac{1}{2}$

   Ⓒ $-7\frac{1}{2}$ or 5

   Ⓓ $-8\frac{2}{3}$ or $3\frac{1}{3}$

4. The variable y varies directly with x, and $y = 8$ when $x = 10$. What is y when $x = 30$?

   Ⓐ 24 Ⓑ 28 Ⓒ 30 Ⓓ 32

5. The best-fitting line for a scatter plot has a slope of 0.25. What is true of the paired data?

   Ⓐ There is a negative correlation.
   Ⓑ There is a positive correlation.
   Ⓒ There is no correlation.
   Ⓓ The data lie on a horizontal line.

6. Create the best fitting line for the scatter plot below. What is a reasonable value for x when $y = 20$?

   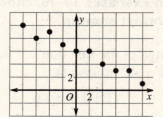

   Ⓐ -40 Ⓑ -24 Ⓒ -4 Ⓓ 10

7. Which function is represented by the graph shown below?

   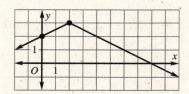

   Ⓐ $y = -2|x - 3| - 2$
   Ⓑ $y = -2|x - 3| + 2$
   Ⓒ $y = -\frac{1}{2}|x - 2| - 3$
   Ⓓ $y = -\frac{1}{2}|x - 2| + 3$

8. Which linear system has many solutions?

   Ⓐ $x - 4y = 9$
   $2x - y = 9$

   Ⓑ $6x + 3y = -2$
   $8x + 4y = -5$

   Ⓒ $-2x + y = 8$
   $2x - y = 4$

   Ⓓ $4x - 3y = 7$
   $-8x + 6y = -14$

9. Which point is *not* a solution of the following system of inequalities?
   $2x - y \geq -4$
   $3x + y \geq -1$

   Ⓐ $(1, 5)$ Ⓑ $(-1, 2)$
   Ⓒ $(-2, -1)$ Ⓓ $(4, -2)$

Post-Course Test continued

10. What is the solution of the system?
$2x + y + z = 5$
$x - y + z = -4$
$x + 2y - z = 10$

- Ⓐ $(1, 4, -1)$
- Ⓑ $(-1, -2, -3)$
- Ⓒ $(1, -4, 7)$
- Ⓓ $(-1, 2, -1)$

11. What is the solution of the matrix equation for x and y?

$$\begin{bmatrix} 5x & 2 \\ -3 & 4y \end{bmatrix} + \begin{bmatrix} -x & -4 \\ 1 & -1 \end{bmatrix} = \begin{bmatrix} -8 & -2 \\ -2 & -5 \end{bmatrix}$$

- Ⓐ $x = 8, y = -1.2$
- Ⓑ $x = -2, y = -1.5$
- Ⓒ $x = -2, y = -1$
- Ⓓ $x = 8, y = -1.5$

12. What is a simplified form of the matrix expression?

$$\begin{bmatrix} 0 & 2 & -1 \\ 3 & 1 & -1 \\ 2 & 0 & 4 \end{bmatrix} \begin{bmatrix} 6 & 4 \\ -1 & 3 \\ 2 & 0 \end{bmatrix}$$

- Ⓐ $\begin{bmatrix} 0 & 8 \\ -3 & 3 \\ 4 & 0 \end{bmatrix}$
- Ⓑ $\begin{bmatrix} -4 & 6 \\ 15 & 15 \\ 20 & 8 \end{bmatrix}$
- Ⓒ $\begin{bmatrix} -4 & 6 \\ -3 & 3 \\ 4 & 8 \end{bmatrix}$
- Ⓓ $\begin{bmatrix} 0 & 6 \\ -3 & 15 \\ 20 & 0 \end{bmatrix}$

13. A triangle has vertices at $A(-5, 2)$, $B(3, 6)$, and $C(1, -4)$. What is the area of the triangle?

- Ⓐ 12 square units
- Ⓑ 18 square units
- Ⓒ 27 square units
- Ⓓ 36 square units

14. What are the zeros of the function $f(x) = 3x^2 + 17x - 6$?

- Ⓐ -3 and 2
- Ⓑ -2 and 3
- Ⓒ -6 and $\frac{1}{3}$
- Ⓓ -6 and 3

15. What is the absolute value of the complex number represented by $\frac{3 + 2i}{1 - i}$?
(*Hint:* First write the expression in standard form.)

- Ⓐ $\sqrt{5}$
- Ⓑ $2\sqrt{5}$
- Ⓒ $\sqrt{26}$
- Ⓓ $\frac{\sqrt{26}}{2}$

16. What are the number and type of solutions of the following equation?
$-9x^2 + 12x - 4 = 0$

- Ⓐ one real
- Ⓑ two real
- Ⓒ one real and one imaginary
- Ⓓ two imaginary

17. A scatter plot of data appears to be quadratic. The x-intercepts are -2.5 and 4, and the y-intercept is 5. What is a quadratic function in standard form for the parabola?

- Ⓐ $y = 2x^2 - x - 20$
- Ⓑ $y = -2x^2 + x + 20$
- Ⓒ $y = -\frac{1}{2}x^2 + \frac{3}{4}x + 5$
- Ⓓ $y = \frac{1}{2}x^2 - \frac{3}{4}x - 5$

Post-Course Test continued

18. What is the sum of the polynomials?

    $$4x^4 + 3x^3 - 5x^2 + 7x - 2$$
    $$+\ 4x^5 + 3x^4 -x^2 - 4x - 1$$

    Ⓐ $4x^5 + 4x^4 + 3x^3 - x^2 + 3x - 3$
    Ⓑ $8x^4 + 6x^3 - 6x^2 + 3x - 3$
    Ⓒ $4x^5 + 7x^4 - 6x^2 + 3x - 3$
    Ⓓ $4x^5 + 7x^4 + 3x^3 - 6x^2 + 3x - 3$

19. The polynomial function $f(x) = 2x^3 - 15x^2 + 6x + 7$ has one zero at $x = 1$. What are the other zeros of $f(x)$?

    Ⓐ $-\frac{1}{2}, -1$, and 7
    Ⓑ $-\frac{1}{2}$ and -1
    Ⓒ $-\frac{1}{2}$ and -7
    Ⓓ $-\frac{1}{2}$ and 7

20. What are the turning points in the graph of $y = \frac{1}{3}x^3 - x^2 - 3x + 1$?

    Ⓐ $(-1, 2\frac{2}{3})$ and $(3, -8)$
    Ⓑ $(-0.21, 0), (0.31, 0)$, and $(4.8, 0)$
    Ⓒ $(-2, \frac{1}{3})$ and $(0, 1)$
    Ⓓ $(1, -2\frac{2}{3})$ and $(4, 4\frac{1}{3})$

21. What is a simplified form of the expression $(-8000)^{2/3}$?

    Ⓐ -400 Ⓑ -20
    Ⓒ 20 Ⓓ 400

22. What is the inverse function of $f(x) = x^2 - 1, x \geq 1$?

    Ⓐ $f^{-1}(x) = \sqrt{x - 1}, x \geq 1$
    Ⓑ $f^{-1}(x) = \sqrt{x + 1}, x \geq 0$
    Ⓒ $f^{-1}(x) = \sqrt{x} - 1, x \geq 1$
    Ⓓ $f^{-1}(x) = \sqrt{x} + 1, x \geq 0$

23. How would you obtain the graph of g from the graph of f?

    $g(x) = 2\sqrt{x - 5}, f(x) = 2\sqrt{x}$

    Ⓐ Shift the graph of f right 5 units.
    Ⓑ Shift the graph of f left 5 units.
    Ⓒ Shift the graph of f up 5 units.
    Ⓓ Shift the graph of f down 5 units.

24. What is the range of the function $y = 2e^{x-4} + 1$?

    Ⓐ $y \geq 3$
    Ⓑ $y \geq 1$
    Ⓒ All real numbers except 3
    Ⓓ All real numbers except 4

25. What is a simplified form of the logarithmic expression $3 \log 2 - \log 4 + \log 6$?

    Ⓐ log 8 Ⓑ log 10
    Ⓒ log 12 Ⓓ log 16

26. What is the solution of the equation $3^{2x} = 27^{x-1}$?

    Ⓐ 0 Ⓑ 1 Ⓒ 2 Ⓓ 3

Post-Course Test continued

27. The number of bacteria in a colony is modeled by the logistic growth function $y = \dfrac{5000}{1 + 20e^{-3.6x}}$. What is the upper bound on the number of bacteria?

    Ⓐ 238 Ⓑ 250 Ⓒ 2500 Ⓓ 5000

28. The variable z varies directly with x and inversely with y. When $x = 4$ and $y = 2$, $z = 4$. What is the value of x when $y = 32$?

    Ⓐ $\dfrac{1}{4}$ Ⓑ $\dfrac{1}{2}$ Ⓒ 4 Ⓓ 8

29. What are the x-intercepts of the graph of the function $y = \dfrac{x^2 + 3x}{x^2 - 4x + 3}$?

    Ⓐ 1 and 3
    Ⓑ 0 and 3
    Ⓒ -3 and 0
    Ⓓ -3 and 3

30. What is a simplified form for the complex fraction $\dfrac{\dfrac{x}{2} - 3}{\dfrac{3}{x} + 1}$?

    Ⓐ $\dfrac{x^2 - 6x}{2x + 6}$ Ⓑ $\dfrac{x^2 - 3x - 18}{2x}$

    Ⓒ $\dfrac{2x - 12}{x}$ Ⓓ $\dfrac{x^2 - 3x + 3}{x + 3}$

31. What is the solution of the equation $\dfrac{4}{x - 6} + 1 = 3$?

    Ⓐ -4 Ⓑ 2 Ⓒ 8 Ⓓ 16

32. What is the approximate distance between $(3, 7)$ and $(8, -14)$?

    Ⓐ 8.6 Ⓑ 14.7 Ⓒ 21.6 Ⓓ 28.3

33. What is the equation for the directrix of the parabola described by $y^2 = 2x$?

    Ⓐ $x = \dfrac{1}{2}$ Ⓑ $x = -\dfrac{1}{2}$

    Ⓒ $x = 8$ Ⓓ $x = -8$

34. What is the radius of the circle described by the equation $x^2 + y^2 - 8x + 2y + 8 = 0$?

    Ⓐ 1 Ⓑ $\sqrt{8}$ Ⓒ 3 Ⓓ 4

35. What are the points of intersection of the graphs in the system?

    $y = x^2 - 7x + 6$
    $y = -\dfrac{1}{2}x + 3$

    Ⓐ $(6, 0)$ and $(1, 2\dfrac{1}{2})$

    Ⓑ $(6, 0)$ and $(\dfrac{1}{2}, 2\dfrac{3}{4})$

    Ⓒ $(-4, 11)$ and $(1, 2\dfrac{1}{2})$

    Ⓓ $(-2, 4)$ and $(4, 1)$

36. What is a rule for the nth term in the sequence?

    $\dfrac{1}{2}, \dfrac{2}{3}, \dfrac{3}{4}, \dfrac{4}{5}, \dfrac{5}{6}, \ldots$

    Ⓐ $a_n = \dfrac{n}{n + 1}$ Ⓑ $a_n = \dfrac{1}{n}$

    Ⓒ $a_n = 1 - \dfrac{1}{n}$ Ⓓ $a_n = 1 - \dfrac{n}{n + 1}$

37. What is the repeating decimal $0.055555\ldots$ written as an infinite geometric series?

    Ⓐ $\sum\limits_{i=1}^{\infty} (0.5)^i$ Ⓑ $\sum\limits_{i=1}^{\infty} (0.5)^{i+1}$

    Ⓒ $\sum\limits_{i=1}^{\infty} 5(0.1)^{i+1}$ Ⓓ $\sum\limits_{i=1}^{\infty} 5(0.5)^{i+1}$

Post-Course Test continued

38. An investment is initially $100,000. Each year it earns 6%, and each year $8000 is withdrawn. How much is it worth after 10 years, to the nearest $1000?
- Ⓐ $70,000
- Ⓑ $74,000
- Ⓒ $78,000
- Ⓓ $99,000

39. Fifteen athletes compete in the 100-meter run. In how many ways can 4 of the athletes place 1st, 2nd, 3rd, and 4th?
- Ⓐ 60
- Ⓑ 8420
- Ⓒ 32,760
- Ⓓ 50,625

40. What is the 6th row of Pascal's triangle? (Count the apex, 1, as the first row.)
- Ⓐ 1 3 6 3 1
- Ⓑ 1 4 6 4 1
- Ⓒ 1 4 9 9 4 1
- Ⓓ 1 5 10 10 5 1

41. Events A and B are mutually exclusive. $P(A) = 0.3$ and $P(B) = 0.2$. What is $P(A \text{ or } B)$?
- Ⓐ 0.1
- Ⓑ 0.5
- Ⓒ 0.6
- Ⓓ 0.7

42. You roll a number cube. If you roll a number greater than 4, you can roll again and add the two rolls together. If you roll a number 4 or less, your turn ends. What is the probability that your total for a turn is 10?
- Ⓐ $\frac{1}{18}$
- Ⓑ $\frac{1}{9}$
- Ⓒ $\frac{1}{6}$
- Ⓓ $\frac{1}{2}$

43. What is the value of x in the right triangle?

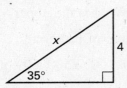

- Ⓐ 2.29 units
- Ⓑ 3.28 units
- Ⓒ 4.88 units
- Ⓓ 6.97 units

44. Which expression is equivalent to $\sin(-120°)$?
- Ⓐ $\sin 60°$
- Ⓑ $\sin 120°$
- Ⓒ $\sin 240°$
- Ⓓ $\sin 330°$

45. What is an xy-equation for the parametric equations?
$y = -5t^2 + 12t + 1$
$x = 3t$
- Ⓐ $y = -\frac{5}{9}x^2 + 4x + 1$
- Ⓑ $y = -45x^2 + 36x + 1$
- Ⓒ $y = -15x^2 + 36x + 1$
- Ⓓ $y = -5x^2 + 15x + 1$

46. What is the amplitude of the graph of the function $y = -3 \cos 4\pi x + 1$?
- Ⓐ -3
- Ⓑ 2
- Ⓒ 3
- Ⓓ 4

47. What is a simplified form of the expression $\sin\left(\frac{\pi}{2} - x\right) \cos(-x)$?
- Ⓐ $\sin^2 x$
- Ⓑ $-\sin^2 x$
- Ⓒ $\cos^2 x$
- Ⓓ $-\cos^2 x$

Test-Taking Tips for Students

For use before the End-of-Course Practice Tests A & B

Test-Taking Strategies

To do a task well, you need both competence and confidence. A person playing the guitar for the first time will not sound like a professional, but even a talented guitarist may perform poorly if he or she is tense and worried.

To perform well on a test, you must have the necessary knowledge and problem-solving skills—you must be *competent* in the subject matter. The most important part of test preparation comes from your everyday work during the school year. If you keep up with your homework, pay attention and ask questions in class, and work to understand each new topic as it comes up, you will develop the knowledge you need to perform well on tests. However, there are strategies that will help you apply your knowledge efficiently and avoid obstacles.

You also need to feel *confident* in your test-taking abilities. While success itself is the best confidence booster, there are some simple things you can do that will help you go into a test feeling relaxed and self-assured.

Before the Test

It is difficult to do well on a test when you are tired, hungry, and nervous. The following strategies will help you be at your best when the test begins.

Take one or more practice tests. Taking a practice test is like rehearsing for a play or going to basketball practice. Practice tests help you understand what the real thing will be like and help you identify areas you may need work on.

Get a full night's sleep. Don't stay up too late the night before an important test, even if you are trying to do last-minute "cramming." A good night's sleep will help you concentrate during the test.

Eat a good breakfast. You need a healthy breakfast to be alert and resourceful during a test, especially a long one.

Be on time, and be prepared. It's hard to do your best on a test when you arrive 5 minutes late and without a pencil. (It's also difficult for your classmates to concentrate while you look for an empty desk!) Being on time will give you a few moments to relax before the test begins.

Choose a good seat. Will you be distracted if you sit near a corner or by your friends? Is there a noisy heater along one wall? Select a comfortable place away from distractions.

Be positive. Try not to be intimidated by a test, even one that is especially important. Go into the room ready to show off how much you know.

During the Test

To do your best on a test, you need to work steadily and efficiently. The following ideas will help you keep on track.

Read questions carefully. Before you begin to answer a question, read it completely. Key information may come at the end of the question. Reread the question if you are not sure you understand what it is asking.

Don't read the answers too soon. Whenever possible, answer the question before looking at the answer choices. Even if you cannot come up with the answer right away, your first try may help you understand the question better and eliminate some answers.

Read all choices before marking your answer. Be sure you know all of your options before choosing an answer. If you are having difficulty understanding a question, the answer choices may help you understand what that question is asking.

Pace yourself. Don't try to go through the test as quickly as you can—this can lead to careless mistakes. Work steadily.

Don't get distracted. Resist the temptation to look up every time you hear a rustling paper or a scooting desk. Focus on *your* paper and *your* thought process.

Don't look for patterns. Especially on standardized tests, there is *no way* to tell what answer comes next by looking at previous answers. Don't waste precious time looking for a pattern that isn't there.

Mark your answer sheet carefully. Take a moment to make sure you mark your answer in the correct place. This is especially important if you skip one or more problems. When answering multiple-choice tests, be sure to fill in the bubble completely and, if you change an answer, to erase all traces of your old mark.

Check your answers. If you have time, go back and check your answers, filling in answers to any problems you may have skipped. *However . . .*

Be SURE before you change an answer. Your first answer is usually your best answer. Don't change an answer unless you are certain the original answer is incorrect.

Test-Taking Tips for Students continued

For use before the End-of-Course Practice Tests A & B

If you get stuck, it is important to stay relaxed and confident even if you struggle with some problems. (Even the best test-takers are stumped occasionally!) The following tips will help you work through any temporary setbacks.

Stay calm. Realize that this is only a small part of the test. Don't let a momentary obstacle affect your confidence.

Don't spend too much time on one problem. If you find a problem especially difficult, move on to others that are easier for you. Make the best guess you can and go on, or skip the problem entirely and return to it later if time permits.

Make an educated guess. If you know some of the answer choices are wrong, eliminate those and make the best guess you can from the rest.

Example A dart thrown at the square target shown is equally likely to hit anywhere inside the target. What is the probability that the dart hits the shaded semicircle?

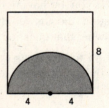

A $\dfrac{\pi}{10}$ **B** $\dfrac{\pi}{8}$

C $\dfrac{\pi}{4}$ **D** $\dfrac{\pi}{2}$

Since you know that no probability can be greater than 1, you may eliminate answer choice **D**, because $\pi \div 2$ is greater than 1.

Even a quick glance will tell you the diagram *has* been drawn to scale. The shaded semicircle seems to be about one-third of the square. The probability therefore must be approximately 0.33. You can eliminate answer choice **C**, since it is equal to approximately 1.

To compute the actual probability, divide the area of the semicircle by the area of the square. The area of the shaded portion is half a circle, or half of πr^2, or 8π, since the radius = 4. The area of the square is 64. The correct choice is **B**.

Work backward. If you are having a difficult time with a problem, you may be able to substitute the answers into the problem and see which one is correct.

Example Which equation is graphed?

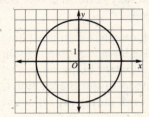

A $x^2 - y^2 = 8 - 2y^2$

B $3x^2 + 3y^2 = 16$

C $4x^2 + 4y^2 = 64$

D $8x^2 + 8y^2 = 16$

To test possible answer choices, recall that $x^2 + y^2 = r^2$ is the formula for a circle with center at the origin and radius r. Therefore $x^2 + y^2 = 16$.

Adding $2y^2$ to each side of answer choice **A** will show that **A** is not correct. A glance at answer choice **B** shows that **B** is not correct. Dividing each side of the equation by 4 in answer choice **C** shows that **C** is the correct answer.

On open-ended problems, be sure your answer covers all that is being asked. Show all of your work and explain your steps or reasoning. Include a diagram if necessary. After you finish your answer, go back and reread the question to make sure you have not left anything out.

After the Test

Reward yourself. If possible, take some time to relax after the test.

Make a plan for the next test. Review what you did before and during the test. Decide which techniques and strategies worked well for you and which ones were not helpful. Think about what you will do differently next time.

Learn from the test. Find out what types of problems caused you the most difficulty and what types you did well on. This will help you prepare for future tests.

Build your confidence for next time. Even if the test did not go well, there are probably some areas where you did succeed. Congratulate yourself on what you did well, and resolve to learn from your mistakes.

Name _____ Date _____

Answer Sheet for Practice Test A

1 Ⓐ Ⓑ Ⓒ Ⓓ	11 Ⓐ Ⓑ Ⓒ Ⓓ	21 Ⓐ Ⓑ Ⓒ Ⓓ	31 Ⓐ Ⓑ Ⓒ Ⓓ	41 Ⓐ Ⓑ Ⓒ Ⓓ	51 Ⓐ Ⓑ Ⓒ Ⓓ
2 Ⓐ Ⓑ Ⓒ Ⓓ	12 Ⓐ Ⓑ Ⓒ Ⓓ	22 Ⓐ Ⓑ Ⓒ Ⓓ	32 Ⓐ Ⓑ Ⓒ Ⓓ	42 Ⓐ Ⓑ Ⓒ Ⓓ	52 Ⓐ Ⓑ Ⓒ Ⓓ
3 Ⓐ Ⓑ Ⓒ Ⓓ	13 Ⓐ Ⓑ Ⓒ Ⓓ	23 Ⓐ Ⓑ Ⓒ Ⓓ	33 Ⓐ Ⓑ Ⓒ Ⓓ	43 Ⓐ Ⓑ Ⓒ Ⓓ	53 Ⓐ Ⓑ Ⓒ Ⓓ
4 Ⓐ Ⓑ Ⓒ Ⓓ	14 Ⓐ Ⓑ Ⓒ Ⓓ	24 Ⓐ Ⓑ Ⓒ Ⓓ	34 Ⓐ Ⓑ Ⓒ Ⓓ	44 Ⓐ Ⓑ Ⓒ Ⓓ	54 Ⓐ Ⓑ Ⓒ Ⓓ
5 Ⓐ Ⓑ Ⓒ Ⓓ	15 Ⓐ Ⓑ Ⓒ Ⓓ	25 Ⓐ Ⓑ Ⓒ Ⓓ	35 Ⓐ Ⓑ Ⓒ Ⓓ	45 Ⓐ Ⓑ Ⓒ Ⓓ	55 Ⓐ Ⓑ Ⓒ Ⓓ
6 Ⓐ Ⓑ Ⓒ Ⓓ	16 Ⓐ Ⓑ Ⓒ Ⓓ	26 Ⓐ Ⓑ Ⓒ Ⓓ	36 Ⓐ Ⓑ Ⓒ Ⓓ	46 Ⓐ Ⓑ Ⓒ Ⓓ	56 Ⓐ Ⓑ Ⓒ Ⓓ
7 Ⓐ Ⓑ Ⓒ Ⓓ	17 Ⓐ Ⓑ Ⓒ Ⓓ	27 Ⓐ Ⓑ Ⓒ Ⓓ	37 Ⓐ Ⓑ Ⓒ Ⓓ	47 Ⓐ Ⓑ Ⓒ Ⓓ	57 Ⓐ Ⓑ Ⓒ Ⓓ
8 Ⓐ Ⓑ Ⓒ Ⓓ	18 Ⓐ Ⓑ Ⓒ Ⓓ	28 Ⓐ Ⓑ Ⓒ Ⓓ	38 Ⓐ Ⓑ Ⓒ Ⓓ	48 Ⓐ Ⓑ Ⓒ Ⓓ	58 Ⓐ Ⓑ Ⓒ Ⓓ
9 Ⓐ Ⓑ Ⓒ Ⓓ	19 Ⓐ Ⓑ Ⓒ Ⓓ	29 Ⓐ Ⓑ Ⓒ Ⓓ	39 Ⓐ Ⓑ Ⓒ Ⓓ	49 Ⓐ Ⓑ Ⓒ Ⓓ	59 Ⓐ Ⓑ Ⓒ Ⓓ
10 Ⓐ Ⓑ Ⓒ Ⓓ	20 Ⓐ Ⓑ Ⓒ Ⓓ	30 Ⓐ Ⓑ Ⓒ Ⓓ	40 Ⓐ Ⓑ Ⓒ Ⓓ	50 Ⓐ Ⓑ Ⓒ Ⓓ	60 Ⓐ Ⓑ Ⓒ Ⓓ

Answer Sheet for Practice Test B

1 Ⓐ Ⓑ Ⓒ Ⓓ	11 Ⓐ Ⓑ Ⓒ Ⓓ	21 Ⓐ Ⓑ Ⓒ Ⓓ	31 Ⓐ Ⓑ Ⓒ Ⓓ	41 Ⓐ Ⓑ Ⓒ Ⓓ	51 Ⓐ Ⓑ Ⓒ Ⓓ
2 Ⓐ Ⓑ Ⓒ Ⓓ	12 Ⓐ Ⓑ Ⓒ Ⓓ	22 Ⓐ Ⓑ Ⓒ Ⓓ	32 Ⓐ Ⓑ Ⓒ Ⓓ	42 Ⓐ Ⓑ Ⓒ Ⓓ	52 Ⓐ Ⓑ Ⓒ Ⓓ
3 Ⓐ Ⓑ Ⓒ Ⓓ	13 Ⓐ Ⓑ Ⓒ Ⓓ	23 Ⓐ Ⓑ Ⓒ Ⓓ	33 Ⓐ Ⓑ Ⓒ Ⓓ	43 Ⓐ Ⓑ Ⓒ Ⓓ	53 Ⓐ Ⓑ Ⓒ Ⓓ
4 Ⓐ Ⓑ Ⓒ Ⓓ	14 Ⓐ Ⓑ Ⓒ Ⓓ	24 Ⓐ Ⓑ Ⓒ Ⓓ	34 Ⓐ Ⓑ Ⓒ Ⓓ	44 Ⓐ Ⓑ Ⓒ Ⓓ	54 Ⓐ Ⓑ Ⓒ Ⓓ
5 Ⓐ Ⓑ Ⓒ Ⓓ	15 Ⓐ Ⓑ Ⓒ Ⓓ	25 Ⓐ Ⓑ Ⓒ Ⓓ	35 Ⓐ Ⓑ Ⓒ Ⓓ	45 Ⓐ Ⓑ Ⓒ Ⓓ	55 Ⓐ Ⓑ Ⓒ Ⓓ
6 Ⓐ Ⓑ Ⓒ Ⓓ	16 Ⓐ Ⓑ Ⓒ Ⓓ	26 Ⓐ Ⓑ Ⓒ Ⓓ	36 Ⓐ Ⓑ Ⓒ Ⓓ	46 Ⓐ Ⓑ Ⓒ Ⓓ	56 Ⓐ Ⓑ Ⓒ Ⓓ
7 Ⓐ Ⓑ Ⓒ Ⓓ	17 Ⓐ Ⓑ Ⓒ Ⓓ	27 Ⓐ Ⓑ Ⓒ Ⓓ	37 Ⓐ Ⓑ Ⓒ Ⓓ	47 Ⓐ Ⓑ Ⓒ Ⓓ	57 Ⓐ Ⓑ Ⓒ Ⓓ
8 Ⓐ Ⓑ Ⓒ Ⓓ	18 Ⓐ Ⓑ Ⓒ Ⓓ	28 Ⓐ Ⓑ Ⓒ Ⓓ	38 Ⓐ Ⓑ Ⓒ Ⓓ	48 Ⓐ Ⓑ Ⓒ Ⓓ	58 Ⓐ Ⓑ Ⓒ Ⓓ
9 Ⓐ Ⓑ Ⓒ Ⓓ	19 Ⓐ Ⓑ Ⓒ Ⓓ	29 Ⓐ Ⓑ Ⓒ Ⓓ	39 Ⓐ Ⓑ Ⓒ Ⓓ	49 Ⓐ Ⓑ Ⓒ Ⓓ	59 Ⓐ Ⓑ Ⓒ Ⓓ
10 Ⓐ Ⓑ Ⓒ Ⓓ	20 Ⓐ Ⓑ Ⓒ Ⓓ	30 Ⓐ Ⓑ Ⓒ Ⓓ	40 Ⓐ Ⓑ Ⓒ Ⓓ	50 Ⓐ Ⓑ Ⓒ Ⓓ	60 Ⓐ Ⓑ Ⓒ Ⓓ

End-of-Course Practice Test A

1. The graph shows the outline of a buried crater. You want to take samples from just inside and just outside the edge of the crater. Which pair of points should you choose?

   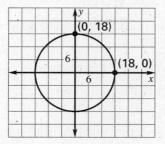

   A (4, 15) and (12, −13)
   B (3, 17) and (−10, −16)
   C (13, −13) and (−8, −17)
   D (−12, 15) and (17, −10)

2. The volume of a square pyramid of height x feet and side length $(10 - x)$ feet is modeled by the equation below.
   $$y = \frac{1}{3}x(10 - x)^2$$
   Use a graphing calculator to graph the function. What is the maximum possible volume of the pyramid?

   A 12.3 ft³
   B 49.4 ft³
   C 122 ft³
   D 667 ft³

3. Rain is falling at a rate of 1.2 centimeters per hour. A cistern system fills at a rate of 2300 liters for every 1.5 centimeters of rain. Use composite functions to find the water added to the cistern after 5 hours of rain.

   A 2760 L
   B 3450 L
   C 9200 L
   D 13,800 L

4. If you rewrite the equation $y = e^{2.39 + 0.62t}$ in standard form $y = ab^t$, what is the base b?

   A 0.54
   B 1.86
   C 2.72
   D 10.9

5. Two pistons are connected to a volume of fluid in a hydraulic system. The force y on the second piston varies directly with the force x on the first piston, as shown in the table.

x	10	15	20	25	30	35
y	378	567	756	945	1134	1323

   What is the approximate force on the second piston when the force on the first piston is 27 pounds?

   A 0.714 lb
   B 954 lb
   C 983 lb
   D 1021 lb

End-of-Course Practice Test A *continued*

6. What are all the vertical asymptotes of the graph of the following function?
$$y = \frac{3x^2 + 7x + 2}{x^2 - 3x - 4}$$
   A $x = -1, x = 4$
   B $x = -4, x = 1$
   C $x = -2, x = -\frac{1}{3}$
   D $x = 2, x = \frac{1}{3}$

7. Use a matrix to solve the system.
   $14.3x - 8.6y = 367.8$
   $21.6x + 15.8y = 138.1$
   A $(34, -13.8)$
   B $(17, -14.5)$
   C $(12, -41)$
   D $(27.5, -29)$

8. What are all the solutions of the equation $|2x - 7| = 35$?
   A 21
   B 14
   C $-21, 14$
   D $-14, 21$

9. The equation describes the distance from a marker on a trail for a jogger who runs to the marker, then turns and runs back.
   $$d = |712.5 - 2.5t|$$
   What does 712.5 represent?
   A the distance she has run when she turns around
   B the total distance she runs
   C the time it takes her to run the whole trail
   D the time she runs until turning around

10. What is $\frac{9 + 2i}{-13 + 6i}$ written as a complex number in standard form?
    A $-\frac{21}{41} - \frac{16}{41}i$
    B $-\frac{105}{133} - \frac{80}{133}i$
    C $-\frac{129}{205} - \frac{16}{41}i$
    D $-\frac{129}{133} - \frac{80}{133}i$

11. What is the maximum value of the function $y = -4.8x^2 + 6.4x - 38.2$?
    A -38.20
    B -36.07
    C -25.47
    D -16.98

12. Which function matches the graph below?

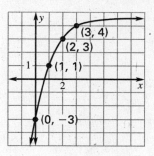

A $y = -4\left(\frac{1}{2}\right)^x + 3$

B $y = -4\left(\frac{1}{2}\right)^{x+1} - 1$

C $y = -4\left(\frac{1}{2}\right)^x + 1$

D $y = -4\left(\frac{1}{2}\right)^{x-1} + 5$

13. A swimming club charges $200 for an individual membership and $3 to park per visit. Which expression could be used to find the average cost per visit after x visits?

A $\dfrac{x}{200 + 3x}$

B $\dfrac{x}{200 - 3x}$

C $\dfrac{200 + 3x}{x}$

D $\dfrac{200 - 3x}{x}$

14. Which is a factor of $x^3 + 64$?

A $x - 4$
B $x + 4$
C $x - 8$
D $x + 8$

15. What is the simplest form of the expression?

$2\sqrt[3]{24} + 5\sqrt[3]{3} + \sqrt[3]{16}$

A $7\sqrt[3]{3}$

B $9\sqrt[3]{3} + 2\sqrt[3]{2}$

C $13\sqrt[3]{3} + 4\sqrt[3]{2}$

D $11\sqrt[3]{6}$

16. What is the upper bound of the graph of the logistic growth function given below?

$y = \dfrac{43.7}{1 + 83.1e^{-2.3x}}$

A $y = 0.526$
B $y = 2.3$
C $y = 43.7$
D $y = 83.1$

17. What is $N - P$?

$N = 0.408x^2 - 1.56x + 39.2$
$P = 0.288x^2 + 3.42x - 0.87$

A $0.12x^2 + 1.86x + 38.33$
B $0.12x^2 + 1.86x + 40.07$
C $0.12x^2 - 4.98x + 38.33$
D $0.12x^2 - 4.98x + 40.07$

End-of-Course Practice Test A continued

18. The scatter plot below shows data that can be modeled with a quadratic function $y = a(x - h)^2 + k$.

    Using the point (3, 29) as the vertex and (7, 20) as another point, what is a good value for a?

    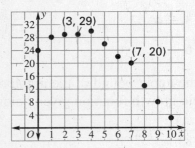

    A -3.06
    B -2.25
    C -0.56
    D -0.29

19. What is the simplified form of the expression $(15^{2/3} \cdot 5^{1/3})^2$?

    A $3^{4/3}$
    B $25 \cdot 3^{4/3}$
    C $5^{2/9} \cdot 3^{2/3}$
    D $5^{2/3} \cdot 3^{4/3}$

20. Use a linear model for the data below to predict $f(20)$.

    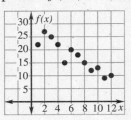

    A -17
    B -8
    C 0
    D 6

21. What is the approximate distance between $(-7, -3)$ and $(9, 8)$?

    A 5.4
    B 11.2
    C 16.8
    D 19.4

22. The variable z varies jointly with x and y. When $x = 14$ and $y = -12$, $z = -8904$. What is z when $x = 22$ and $y = 9$?

    A 198
    B 10,494
    C 15,120
    D 33,264

23. What is an equation of the circle shown below?

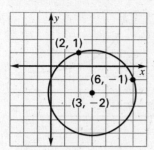

A $(x + 3)^2 + (y - 2)^2 = 10$
B $(x + 3)^2 + (y - 2)^2 = \sqrt{10}$
C $(x - 3)^2 + (y + 2)^2 = 10$
D $(x - 2)^2 + (y + 2)^2 = \sqrt{10}$

24. What is the solution of
$\frac{3(x-2)}{x} + 1 = \frac{2(x+3)}{x}$?

A 2.5
B 4
C 6
D 11

25. The volume of a sphere is given by $V = \frac{4}{3}\pi r^3$, where r is the radius of the sphere. What is an approximate value of r when $V = 3370$ cubic inches?

A 9.3 in.
B 13.6 in.
C 20.0 in.
D 28.4 in.

26. Perform the indicated operations.
$3 \begin{bmatrix} 8 & 0 \\ -12 & 15 \end{bmatrix} - \begin{bmatrix} 17 & 26 \\ 38 & -52 \end{bmatrix}$

A $\begin{bmatrix} 7 & -26 \\ 2 & -7 \end{bmatrix}$

B $\begin{bmatrix} 7 & -26 \\ -74 & 97 \end{bmatrix}$

C $\begin{bmatrix} 24 & 0 \\ -36 & 45 \end{bmatrix}$

D $\begin{bmatrix} 17 & -26 \\ -74 & -97 \end{bmatrix}$

27. What are the factors of the expression $x^4 - 25x^2 + 144$?

A $(x - 6)(x + 2)(x - 4)(x + 3)$
B $(x - 5)(x + 5)(x - 4)(x + 4)$
C $(x^2 + 9)(x - 4)(x + 4)$
D $(x - 3)(x + 3)(x - 4)(x + 4)$

28. Which inequality is graphed below?

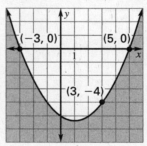

A $y \le \frac{1}{3}x^2 + \frac{2}{3}x - 5$

B $y \le \frac{1}{3}x^2 - \frac{2}{3}x - 5$

C $y \le \frac{2}{3}x^2 + \frac{4}{3}x - 5$

D $y \le \frac{2}{3}x^2 - \frac{4}{3}x - 5$

End-of-Course Practice Test A continued

29. You deposit $3500 in an account that pays 4% annual interest compounded continuously. What is the balance after 8 years?

   A $4761.71
   B $4789.99
   C $4819.95
   D $8042.68

30. What is the solution of $8x^4 - 5 = 19$? Round to two decimal places.

   A ±0.28
   B ±1.15
   C ±1.32
   D ±2.21

31. What is the absolute value of the complex number graphed below?

   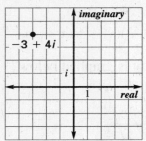

   A $\sqrt{7}$
   B 4
   C $\sqrt{12}$
   D 5

32. What are all the asymptotes of the rational function graphed below?

   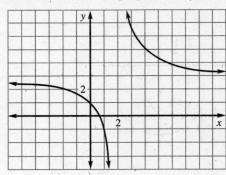

   A $x = 2, y = 3$
   B $x = 1, y = 4$
   C $x = 3, y = 3$
   D $x = 1, y = 3$

33. What is the inverse function of $f(x) = 8x^3 + 3$?

   A $f^{-1}(x) = \dfrac{\sqrt[3]{x-3}}{2}$
   B $f^{-1}(x) = \sqrt[3]{\dfrac{x-3}{2}}$
   C $f^{-1}(x) = \sqrt[3]{\dfrac{x}{2}} - 3$
   D $f^{-1}(x) = \dfrac{\sqrt[3]{x}}{2} - 3$

34. Which ordered pair is a solution of the system of inequalities below?
   $-4x + 2y > 1$
   $x + 3y < 12$

   A $(-7, 7)$
   B $(-2, 8)$
   C $(-4, 5)$
   D $(-1, -3)$

35. What is the area of the triangle shown below?

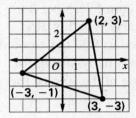

- A 16
- B 17
- C 18
- D 19

36. Find an exponential model of the form $f(x) = ab^x$ for a graph that passes through the points (2, 45) and (5, 1215). What is $f(4)$ using this model?

- A 60
- B 295
- C 405
- D 50,625

37. If a weight on the end of a string is spun in a circle with a force of F newtons, its speed v, in meters per second, is given by the following formula, where m is the mass in kilograms and r is the radius in meters.

$$v = \sqrt{\frac{Fr}{m}}$$

A 0.04 kilogram weight is attached to a 3 meter string and spun with a force of 10.45 newtons. What is the approximate speed?

- A 12 m/sec
- B 17 m/sec
- C 24 m/sec
- D 28 m/sec

38. What is the equation of the graph of an absolute value function that opens down with vertex (4, 1) and passes through the point (6, 0)?

- A $y = \frac{1}{2}|x - 4| + 1$
- B $y = -\frac{1}{2}|x - 4| + 1$
- C $y = 2|x - 4| + 1$
- D $y = -2|x - 4| + 1$

End-of-Course Practice Test A *continued*

39. A parabola has its vertex at (0, 0) and focus at $(0, -1\frac{1}{4})$. What is the standard form of the equation of the parabola?

  A $x^2 = 5y$
  B $x^2 = -5y$
  C $x^2 = 1\frac{1}{4}y$
  D $x^2 = -1\frac{1}{4}y$

40. What is the simplified form of the expression $3x^2 + 5(x - 1) - 2x(3 - x)$?

  A $-x^2 + 7x - 5$
  B $-3x^2 + 5x - 5$
  C $5x^2 - x - 5$
  D $x^2 - x - 5$

41. Rebecca earns $6 per hour baby-sitting, while Tomás earns $5.50 per hour baby-sitting. Both earn $7.25 per hour working at the library. Which matrix model could be used to find the amount they would each earn baby-sitting for 5 hours and working at the library for 12 hours?

  A $\begin{bmatrix} 5 \\ 12 \end{bmatrix} \begin{bmatrix} 6 & 5.5 \\ 7.25 & 7.25 \end{bmatrix}$

  B $\begin{bmatrix} 5 \\ 12 \end{bmatrix} \begin{bmatrix} 6 & 7.25 \\ 5.5 & 7.25 \end{bmatrix}$

  C $\begin{bmatrix} 6 & 5.5 \\ 7.25 & 7.25 \end{bmatrix} \begin{bmatrix} 5 \\ 12 \end{bmatrix}$

  D $\begin{bmatrix} 6 & 7.25 \\ 5.5 & 7.25 \end{bmatrix} \begin{bmatrix} 5 \\ 12 \end{bmatrix}$

42. What are the points of intersection of the graphs of the equations?

  $x - 3y = -10$
  $x^2 + y^2 = 20$

  A $(-2, -4)$ and $(2, -4)$
  B $(2, 4)$ and $(4, 2)$
  C $(2, 4)$ and $(-4, 2)$
  D $(2, -4)$ and $(4, 2)$

End-of-Course Practice Test A *continued*

43. You need to evaluate $\log_3 85$, but your calculator can only find logarithms of base 10 or base e. How can you rewrite the equation to find $\log_3 85$ using base 10 logarithms?

   A $(\log_{10} 85)(\log_{10} 3)$

   B $\dfrac{\log_{10} 85}{\log_{10} 3}$

   C $\log_{10} 85 - \log_{10} 3$

   D $\log_{10} (85^3)$

44. Trey runs at a steady rate of 5 feet per second until he reaches the corner of the field, then turns and runs back. His distance from his starting point can be modeled by the function below, where y is the distance in feet and x is the time in seconds.

   $y = -5|x - 24| + 120$

   After how many seconds did he reach the corner of the field?

   A 5 sec

   B 24 sec

   C 60 sec

   D 120 sec

45. The graph shows the weights of several children between 0 and 12 months of age. Which linear model is the best fit for the data?

   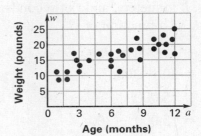

   A $w = 1.5a + 12$

   B $w = 2.3a + 7$

   C $w = 1.1a + 8$

   D $w = 0.8a + 5$

46. What is the solution of the linear system?
   $3x + 2y = -13$
   $-x + 2y = 15$

   A $(-7, 4)$

   B $(-8, 12)$

   C $(1, 8)$

   D $(1, -8)$

47. What are the x-intercepts of the rational function below?

   $y = \dfrac{x^2 + 2x - 24}{2x^2 + 7x - 15}$

   A -6 and 4

   B 5 and $1\frac{1}{2}$

   C -4 and 6

   D $-1\frac{1}{2}$ and 5

End-of-Course Practice Test A *continued*

48. The gravitational potential energy U of a rock climber at a height h is given by $U(h) = 500h$. The climber's height is given by $h(t) = 30 - 0.6t$. U is measured in Joules, h in meters, and t in seconds. What is U as a function of t?

 A $U(t) = 15{,}000 - 0.6t$
 B $U(t) = 30 - 300t$
 C $U(t) = 15{,}000t$
 D $U(t) = 15{,}000 - 300t$

49. Using the relation below, what is x when $y = 8$?

$$y = \frac{1}{8}2^x$$

 A 4
 B 6
 C 8
 D 10

50. The graph shows the outline of a sunken garden. What equation describes the circle?

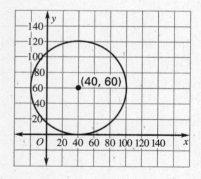

 A $(x - 20)^2 + (y - 30)^2 = 30^2$
 B $(x - 20)^2 + (y - 30)^2 = 20^2$
 C $(x - 40)^2 + (y - 60)^2 = 60^2$
 D $(x - 40)^2 + (y - 60)^2 = 40^2$

51. What is the solution of the inequality $|14 - 3x| < 20$ for x?

 A $-2 < x < 11\frac{1}{3}$
 B $-11\frac{1}{3} < x < 2$
 C $x < -2$ or $x > 11\frac{1}{3}$
 D $x < -11\frac{1}{3}$ or $x > 2$

52. What is the expression written as a complex number in standard form?

$(12 + 3i)(-5 + 4i)$

 A $-60 + 12i$
 B $-48 + 33i$
 C $-72 + 33i$
 D $-52 + 17i$

53. A simple pendulum of length x meters takes $2\sqrt{x}$ seconds to swing back and forth. How long is a pendulum that takes 0.8 seconds to swing back and forth?

 A 0.63 m
 B 0.40 m
 C 0.20 m
 D 0.16 m

End-of-Course Practice Test A *continued*

54. Matrix Q represents the in-season and off-season costs per night of 2 different room sizes at a resort. Matrix R represents the number of rooms of each size the Green and Wong parties need. Which matrix below correctly shows the costs per night for both groups in- and off-season?

$$Q = \begin{array}{c} \text{off-season} \\ \text{in-season} \end{array} \begin{array}{cc} \text{1 bed} & \text{2 beds} \\ \begin{bmatrix} 75 & 100 \\ 120 & 150 \end{bmatrix} \end{array}$$

$$R = \begin{array}{c} \text{1 bed} \\ \text{2 beds} \end{array} \begin{array}{cc} \text{Green} & \text{Wong} \\ \begin{bmatrix} 2 & 0 \\ 1 & 3 \end{bmatrix} \end{array}$$

A $\begin{array}{c} \text{off-season} \\ \text{in-season} \end{array} \begin{array}{cc} \text{Green} & \text{Wong} \\ \begin{bmatrix} 250 & 300 \\ 390 & 450 \end{bmatrix} \end{array}$

B $\begin{array}{c} \text{off-season} \\ \text{in-season} \end{array} \begin{array}{cc} \text{Green} & \text{Wong} \\ \begin{bmatrix} 150 & 100 \\ 240 & 300 \end{bmatrix} \end{array}$

C $\begin{array}{c} \text{off-season} \\ \text{in-season} \end{array} \begin{array}{cc} \text{Green} & \text{Wong} \\ \begin{bmatrix} 150 & 200 \\ 435 & 550 \end{bmatrix} \end{array}$

D $\begin{array}{c} \text{off-season} \\ \text{in-season} \end{array} \begin{array}{cc} \text{Green} & \text{Wong} \\ \begin{bmatrix} 250 & 300 \\ 240 & 360 \end{bmatrix} \end{array}$

55. The capacitance C of a capacitor varies inversely with the electric potential difference ΔV and varies directly with the charge q. Which formula is correct?

A $C = q - \Delta V$

B $C = q(\Delta V)$

C $C = \dfrac{\Delta V}{q}$

D $C = \dfrac{q}{\Delta V}$

56. Which function describes this graph?

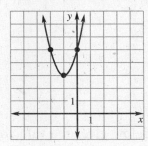

A $y = 2(x - 1)^2 + 3$

B $y = 2(x + 1)^2 + 3$

C $y = 2(x - 3)^2 + 1$

D $y = 2(x + 3)^2 - 1$

57. The graph of a cubic function of the form $y = ax^3 + b$ is shown below. What can you determine about the values of a and b?

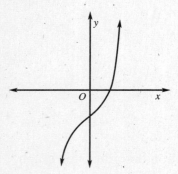

- **A** $a > 0, b > 0$
- **B** $a > 0, b < 0$
- **C** $a < 0, b > 0$
- **D** $a < 0, b < 0$

58. The expression below gives the value of the voltage in a circuit with current I and 2 parallel resistors with resistances R and $3R$. What is the simplified form of the fraction?

$$\frac{I}{\frac{1}{R} + \frac{1}{3R}}$$

- **A** $4IR$
- **B** $\dfrac{4I}{3R}$
- **C** $\dfrac{3IR}{4}$
- **D** $\dfrac{3I}{R}$

59. The height of a ball thrown straight up into the air with velocity 4 meters per second can be modeled by the equation $h = -5t^2 + 4t + 2$, where h is the height in meters and t is the time in seconds. What does the constant term 2 indicate?

- **A** The ball is thrown from 2 meters above the ground.
- **B** The ball falls at a rate of 2 meters per second.
- **C** The ball's maximum height is 2 meters.
- **D** The ball reaches its highest point after 2 seconds.

60. A reflecting pool measuring 20 feet by 8 feet is to be surrounded by tiles in a border x feet wide. The garden designer can spend $1500 on tiles. Which expression represents the maximum cost per square foot of tile?

- **A** $\dfrac{1500}{(2x + 20)(2x + 8)}$
- **B** $\dfrac{1500}{20(8) - (2x + 20)(2x + 8)}$
- **C** $\dfrac{1500}{(2x + 20)(2x + 8) - 20(8)}$
- **D** $\dfrac{1500}{20(8)x^2}$

End-of-Course Practice Test B

1. The graph shows the outline of a buried crater. You want to take samples from just inside and just outside the edge of the crater. Which pair of points should you choose?

   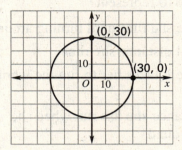

   A $(8, -26)$ and $(17, 20)$
   B $(-15, 15)$ and $(23, 9)$
   C $(16, 27)$ and $(10, -29)$
   D $(5, 28)$ and $(20, -25)$

2. The volume of a square pyramid of height x feet and side length $(9 - x)$ feet is modeled by the equation below.

   $$y = \frac{1}{3}x(9 - x)^2$$

   Use a graphing calculator to graph the function. What is the maximum possible volume of the pyramid?

   A 36 ft^3
   B 42 ft^3
   C 51 ft^3
   D 63 ft^3

3. Rain is falling at a rate of 1.6 centimeters per hour. A cistern system fills at a rate of 4200 liters for every 1.2 centimeters of rain. Use composite functions to find the water added to the cistern after 5 hours of rain.

   A 5600 L
   B 14,800 L
   C 28,000 L
   D 33,600 L

4. If you rewrite the equation $y = e^{4.83 + 0.19t}$ in standard form $y = ab^t$, what is the base b?

   A 1.21
   B 15.3
   C 125.2
   D 151.4

5. Two pistons are connected to a volume of fluid in a hydraulic system. The force y on the second piston varies directly with the force x on the first piston as shown in the table.

x	15	20	25	30	35
y	126	168	210	252	294

   What is the approximate force on the second piston when the force on the first piston is 32 pounds?

   A 3.8 lb
   B 129 lb
   C 269 lb
   D 283 lb

End-of-Course Practice Test B *continued*

6. What are all the vertical asymptotes of the graph of the following function?

   $$y = \frac{2x^2 + 6x - 8}{x^2 - 2x - 15}$$

   A $x = -3, x = 5$
   B $x = 3, x = -5$
   C $x = -4, x = 1$
   D $x = 4, x = -1$

7. Use a matrix to solve the system.

   $3.2x - 7.4y = 110.9$
   $12.2x + 6y = 132$

   A $(19, -6.8)$
   B $(12, -9.8)$
   C $(15, -8.5)$
   D $(13, -4.5)$

8. What are all the solutions of the equation $|2x + 13| = 25$?

   A 6
   B 19
   C 6, −19
   D −6, 17

9. The equation describes the distance from a marker on a trail for a jogger who runs to the marker, then turns and runs back.

   $d = |810 - 2.25t|$

   What does 810 represent?

   A the time she runs until turning around
   B the total distance she runs
   C the time it takes her to run the whole trail
   D the distance she has run when she turns around

10. What is $\dfrac{8 - 3i}{6 + 5i}$ written as a complex number in standard form?

    A $3 - \dfrac{58}{11}i$
    B $\dfrac{33}{61} - \dfrac{58}{61}i$
    C $\dfrac{63}{11} - \dfrac{58}{11}i$
    D $\dfrac{63}{61} - \dfrac{58}{61}i$

11. What is the maximum value of the function $y = -6.5x^2 + 28.6x - 22.4$?

    A 3.28
    B 5.20
    C 8.37
    D 9.06

End-of-Course Practice Test B *continued*

12. Which function matches the graph below?

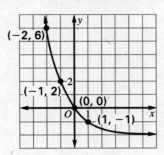

- **A** $y = 4\left(\dfrac{1}{2}\right)^{x+1} - 2$
- **B** $y = 4\left(\dfrac{1}{2}\right)^{x} - 4$
- **C** $y = 4\left(\dfrac{1}{2}\right)^{x} - 3$
- **D** $y = 4\left(\dfrac{1}{2}\right)^{x-1} - 8$

13. A museum charges $145 for a family membership. Parking at the museum costs $9 per visit. Which expression could be used to find the average cost per visit after x visits?

- **A** $\dfrac{145 - 9x}{x}$
- **B** $\dfrac{145 + 9x}{x}$
- **C** $\dfrac{x}{145 - 9x}$
- **D** $\dfrac{x}{145 + 9x}$

14. Which is a factor of $x^3 + 125$?

- **A** $x + 5$
- **B** $x - 5$
- **C** $x + 25$
- **D** $x - 25$

15. What is the simplest form of the expression?

$$\sqrt[3]{25} + \sqrt[3]{200} - \sqrt[3]{5}$$

- **A** $17\sqrt[3]{5}$
- **B** $15 - \sqrt[3]{5}$
- **C** $9\sqrt[3]{25} - \sqrt[3]{5}$
- **D** $3\sqrt[3]{25} - \sqrt[3]{5}$

16. What is the upper bound of the graph of the logistic growth function given below?

$$y = \dfrac{23.8}{1 + 62.7e^{-0.81x}}$$

- **A** $y = 0.38$
- **B** $y = 0.82$
- **C** $y = 23.8$
- **D** $y = 62.7$

17. What is $N - P$?

$N = 1.301x^2 + 0.48x - 81.2$
$P = 0.497x^2 - 5.61x + 32.5$

- **A** $0.804x^2 + 6.09x - 48.7$
- **B** $0.804x^2 - 5.13x - 113.7$
- **C** $0.804x^2 - 5.13x - 48.7$
- **D** $0.804x^2 + 6.09x - 113.7$

End-of-Course Practice Test B *continued*

18. The scatter plot below shows data that can be modeled with a quadratic function, $y = a(x - h)^2 + k$.

Using the point (3, 37) as the vertex and (1, 14) as another point, what is a good value for a?

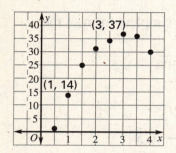

- A -23
- B -13.2
- C -5.75
- D -0.29

19. What is the simplified form of the expression $(8^{3/4} \cdot 2^{1/4})^2$?

- A 32
- B $8^{1/4} \cdot 2^{1/2}$
- C $2^{5/2}$
- D 64

20. Use a linear model for the data below to predict $f(12)$.

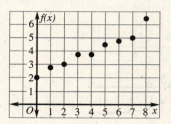

- A 7
- B 8
- C 10
- D 13

21. What is the approximate distance between $(-4, 17)$ and $(6, -21)$?

- A 11.2
- B 28.4
- C 37.4
- D 39.3

22. The variable z varies jointly with x and y. When $x = 9$ and $y = 15$, $z = 5805$. What is z when $x = 13$ and $y = 6$?

- A 3354
- B 3870
- C 4232
- D 5031

End-of-Course Practice Test B continued

23. What is an equation of the circle shown below?

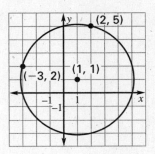

A $(x - 1)^2 + (y - 1)^2 = 17$
B $(x - 1)^2 + (y - 1)^2 = \sqrt{17}$
C $(x - 3)^2 + (y + 2)^2 = 17$
D $(x - 3)^2 + (y + 2)^2 = \sqrt{17}$

24. What is the solution of
$\frac{2x}{x+1} - 4 = 2\frac{(x-5)}{x+1}$?

A 0
B 1.5
C 2
D 4

25. The volume of a sphere is given by $V = \frac{4}{3}\pi r^3$, where r is the radius of the sphere. What is an approximate value of r when $V = 26{,}090$ cubic centimeters?

A 18.4 cm
B 22.3 cm
C 32.8 cm
D 47.8 cm

26. Perform the indicated operations.
$\begin{bmatrix} 8 & -3 \\ 1 & 12 \end{bmatrix} + 4 \begin{bmatrix} -1 & 7 \\ 5 & -7 \end{bmatrix}$

A $\begin{bmatrix} 12 & -31 \\ 20 & -26 \end{bmatrix}$

B $\begin{bmatrix} 4 & -31 \\ 20 & -26 \end{bmatrix}$

C $\begin{bmatrix} 12 & 25 \\ 21 & -14 \end{bmatrix}$

D $\begin{bmatrix} 4 & 25 \\ 21 & -16 \end{bmatrix}$

27. What are the factors of the expression $x^4 - 41x^2 + 400$?

A $(x + 4)(x + 4)(x - 5)(x - 5)$
B $(x - 10)(x + 10)(x - 2)(x + 2)$
C $(x^2 + 25)(x - 4)(x + 4)$
D $(x + 4)(x - 4)(x + 5)(x - 5)$

End-of-Course Practice Test B continued

28. Which inequality is graphed below?

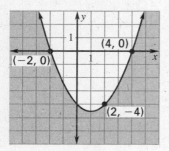

A $y \le \frac{1}{2}x^2 + x - 4$

B $y \le \frac{1}{2}x^2 - x - 4$

C $y \le \frac{1}{4}x^2 + \frac{1}{2}x - 4$

D $y \le \frac{1}{4}x^2 - x - 4$

29. You deposit $5200 in an account that pays 3% annual interest compounded continuously. What is the balance after 12 years?

   A $7305.63
   B $7413.96
   C $7453.31
   D $7516.41

30. Given that $x > 0$, what is the solution of $41 = 6x^3 + 1$? Round to two decimal places.

   A 1.88
   B 2.58
   C 3.42
   D 3.55

31. What is the absolute value of the complex number graphed below?

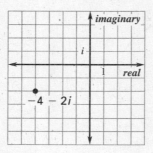

   A $\sqrt{2}$
   B 2
   C 4
   D $2\sqrt{5}$

32. What are all the asymptotes of the rational function graphed below?

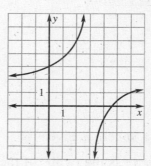

   A $x = 2, y = 3$
   B $x = 3, y = 2$
   C $x = 4, y = 3$
   D $x = 2, y = 2$

End-of-Course Practice Test B continued

33. What is the inverse function of $f(x) = 3x^3 - 6$?

    A $f^{-1}(x) = \sqrt[3]{\dfrac{x}{3}} + 2$

    B $f^{-1}(x) = \sqrt[3]{\dfrac{x}{3} + 2}$

    C $f^{-1}(x) = \sqrt[3]{\dfrac{x+2}{3}}$

    D $f^{-1}(x) = 2\sqrt[3]{\dfrac{x}{3}}$

34. Which ordered pair is a solution of the system of inequalities below?

    $2x - y > 1$
    $x + y < 2$

    A $(-1, 1)$
    B $(4, 1)$
    C $(3, -3)$
    D $(-5, -4)$

35. What is the area of the triangle shown below?

    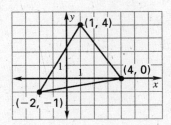

    A 13
    B 13.5
    C 14
    D 14.5

36. Find an exponential model of the form $f(x) = ab^x$ for a graph that passes through the points (2, 1215) and (4, 98,415). What is $f(3)$ using this model?

    A 4265
    B 9875
    C 10,935
    D 30,375

37. If a weight on the end of a string is spun in a circle with a force of F newtons, its speed v, in meters per second, is given by the following formula, where m is the mass in kilograms and r is the radius in meters.

    $$v = \sqrt{\dfrac{Fr}{m}}$$

    A 0.025 kilogram weight is attached to a 1.2 meter string and spun with a force of 4.7 newtons. What is the approximate speed?

    A 0.38 m/sec
    B 15 m/sec
    C 42 m/sec
    D 95 m/sec

End-of-Course Practice Test B *continued*

38. What is the equation of the graph of an absolute value function that opens down with vertex (−3, 1) and passes through the point (0, 0)?

   A $y = \frac{1}{3}|x - 1| + 3$

   B $y = \frac{1}{3}|x - 3| + 1$

   C $y = -\frac{1}{3}|x - 3| + 3$

   D $y = -\frac{1}{3}|x + 3| + 1$

39. A parabola has its vertex at (0, 0) and focus at $\left(1\frac{1}{2}, 0\right)$. What is the standard form of the equation of the parabola?

   A $y^2 = -\frac{3}{2}x$

   B $y^2 = -6x$

   C $y^2 = \frac{3}{2}x$

   D $y^2 = 6x$

40. What is the simplified form of the expression $x^2 + 3(3x - 4) - 2x(6 + 2x)$?

   A $5x^2 - 3x - 12$

   B $-3x^2 - 3x - 12$

   C $5x^2 + 3x - 12$

   D $-3x^2 + 3x - 12$

41. Leann earns $5.00 per hour baby-sitting, while Sara earns $5.50 per hour baby-sitting. Both earn $7.50 per hour working at the library. Which matrix model could be used to find the amount they would each earn baby-sitting for 6 hours and working at the library for 10 hours?

   A $\begin{bmatrix} 5 & 7.5 \\ 5.5 & 7.5 \end{bmatrix} \begin{bmatrix} 6 \\ 10 \end{bmatrix}$

   B $\begin{bmatrix} 6 \\ 10 \end{bmatrix} \begin{bmatrix} 5 & 7.5 \\ 5.5 & 7.5 \end{bmatrix}$

   C $\begin{bmatrix} 5 & 5.5 \\ 7.5 & 7.5 \end{bmatrix} \begin{bmatrix} 6 \\ 10 \end{bmatrix}$

   D $\begin{bmatrix} 6 \\ 10 \end{bmatrix} \begin{bmatrix} 5 & 5.5 \\ 7.5 & 7.5 \end{bmatrix}$

42. What are the points of intersection of the graphs of the equations?

   $-x + 7y = 25$
   $x^2 + y^2 = 25$

   A (4, 3) and (−3, −4)

   B (4, −3) and (−3, 4)

   C (3, 4) and (−3, −4)

   D (3, 4) and (−4, 3)

End-of-Course Practice Test B continued

43. You need to evaluate $\log_7 205$, but your calculator can only find logarithms of base 10 or base e. How can you rewrite the equation to find $\log_7 205$ using base 10 logarithms?

   A $(\log_{10} 205)(\log_{10} 7)$
   B $\log_{10}(205^7)$
   C $\log_{10} 205 - \log_{10} 7$
   D $\dfrac{\log_{10} 205}{\log_{10} 7}$

44. Joanna runs at a steady rate of 6 feet per second until she reaches the end of the block, then turns and runs back. Her distance from the starting point can be modeled by the function below, where y is the distance in feet and x is the time in seconds.

   $y = -6|x - 40| + 240$

   After how many seconds did she reach the end of the block?

   A 6 sec
   B 24 sec
   C 40 sec
   D 240 sec

45. The graph shows the number of test questions from each chapter on an exam. Which linear model is the best fit for the data?

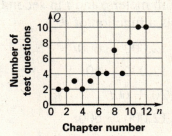

   A $Q = 1.5n + 2$
   B $Q = 0.5n$
   C $Q = n + 2$
   D $Q = 0.8n + 0.5$

46. What is the solution of the linear system?

   $2x - 5y = 11$
   $x + 2y = 1$

   A $(3, -1)$
   B $(-2, -3)$
   C $(5, -2)$
   D $(8, 1)$

47. What are the x-intercepts of the rational function below?

   $y = \dfrac{2x^2 - 5x - 12}{x^2 - x - 2}$

   A $-1\frac{1}{2}$ and 4
   B -1 and 2
   C -4 and $1\frac{1}{2}$
   D -2 and 1

End-of-Course Practice Test B *continued*

48. The gravitational potential energy U of a rock climber at a height h is given by $U(h) = 600h$. The climber's height is given by $h(t) = 20 + 0.1t$. U is measured in Joules, h in meters, and t in seconds. What is U as a function of t?

   A $U(t) = 12{,}000 + 600t$
   B $U(t) = 12{,}000 + 60t$
   C $U(t) = 20 + 60t$
   D $U(t) = 12{,}000 - 600t$

49. Using the relation below, what is x when $y = 3$?

   $y = \frac{1}{9}3^x$

   A -2
   B 1
   C 3
   D 27

50. The graph shows the outline of a sunken garden. What equation describes the circle?

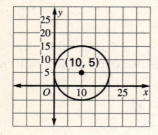

   A $(x - 10)^2 + (y - 5)^2 = 10^2$
   B $(x - 10)^2 + (y - 5)^2 = 5^2$
   C $(x - 5)^2 + (y - 10)^2 = 10^2$
   D $(x - 5)^2 + (y - 10)^2 = 5^2$

51. What is the solution of the inequality $|6 + 2x| > 1$ for x?

   A $2\frac{1}{2} < x < 3\frac{1}{2}$
   B $-3\frac{1}{2} < x < -2\frac{1}{2}$
   C $x < -3\frac{1}{2}$ or $x > -2\frac{1}{2}$
   D $x < 2\frac{1}{2}$ or $x > 3\frac{1}{2}$

52. What is the expression written as a complex number in standard form?

   $(6 - 8i)(2 + i)$

   A $20 - 10i$
   B $12 - 16i$
   C $12 - 10i$
   D $20 - 24i$

53. A simple pendulum of length x meters takes $2\sqrt{x}$ seconds to swing back and forth. How long is a pendulum that takes 0.6 seconds to swing back and forth?

   A 0.155 m
   B 0.09 m
   C 0.9 m
   D 1.44 m

End-of-Course Practice Test B *continued*

54. Matrix Q represents the costs per night of 2 different room sizes at a resort in-season and off-season. Matrix R represents the number of rooms of each size the Lo and Ransom parties need. Which matrix below correctly shows the costs per night for both groups in- and off-season?

$$Q = \begin{matrix} \text{off-season} \\ \text{in-season} \end{matrix} \begin{matrix} \text{1 bed} & \text{2 beds} \\ \begin{bmatrix} 100 & 150 \\ 125 & 200 \end{bmatrix} \end{matrix}$$

$$R = \begin{matrix} \text{1 bed} \\ \text{2 beds} \end{matrix} \begin{matrix} \text{Lo} & \text{Ransom} \\ \begin{bmatrix} 3 & 2 \\ 0 & 2 \end{bmatrix} \end{matrix}$$

A $\begin{matrix} \text{off-season} \\ \text{in-season} \end{matrix} \begin{matrix} \text{Lo} & \text{Ransom} \\ \begin{bmatrix} 550 & 850 \\ 250 & 400 \end{bmatrix} \end{matrix}$

B $\begin{matrix} \text{off-season} \\ \text{in-season} \end{matrix} \begin{matrix} \text{Lo} & \text{Ransom} \\ \begin{bmatrix} 300 & 500 \\ 375 & 650 \end{bmatrix} \end{matrix}$

C $\begin{matrix} \text{off-season} \\ \text{in-season} \end{matrix} \begin{matrix} \text{Lo} & \text{Ransom} \\ \begin{bmatrix} 300 & 300 \\ 250 & 400 \end{bmatrix} \end{matrix}$

D $\begin{matrix} \text{off-season} \\ \text{in-season} \end{matrix} \begin{matrix} \text{Lo} & \text{Ransom} \\ \begin{bmatrix} 400 & 850 \\ 375 & 650 \end{bmatrix} \end{matrix}$

55. The electric potential difference ΔV on a capacitor varies inversely with the capacitance C and varies directly with the charge q. Which formula is correct?

A $\Delta V = \dfrac{C}{q}$

B $\Delta V = \dfrac{q}{C}$

C $\Delta V = q - C$

D $\Delta V = q(C)$

56. Which function describes this graph?

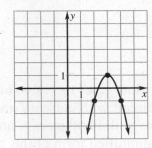

A $y = -2(x - 1)^2 + 3$
B $y = 2(x + 1)^2 + 3$
C $y = -2(x - 3)^2 + 1$
D $y = 2(x + 3)^2 - 1$

End-of-Course Practice Test B *continued*

57. The graph of a cubic function of the form $y = ax^3 + b$ is shown below. What can you determine about the values of a and b?

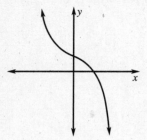

- A $a > 0, b > 0$
- B $a > 0, b < 0$
- C $a < 0, b > 0$
- D $a < 0, b < 0$

58. The expression below gives the value of the voltage in a circuit with current I and 2 parallel resistors with resistances R and $5R$. What is the simplified form of the fraction?

$$\frac{I}{\frac{1}{R} + \frac{1}{5R}}$$

- A $5IR$
- B $\frac{6I}{5R}$
- C $\frac{6I}{R}$
- D $\frac{5IR}{6}$

59. The height of a ball thrown straight up into the air with velocity 6 meters per second can be modeled by the equation $h = -5t^2 + 6t + 1$, where h is the height in meters and t is the time in seconds. What does the constant term 1 indicate?

- A The ball is thrown from 1 meter above the ground.
- B The ball falls at a rate of 1 meter per second.
- C The ball reaches its highest point after 1 second.
- D The ball's maximum height is 1 meter.

60. A reflecting pool measuring 15 feet by 9 feet is to be surrounded by tiles in a border x feet wide. The garden designer can spend $2000 on tiles. Which expression represents the maximum cost per square foot of tile?

- A $\dfrac{2000}{(2x + 15)(2x + 9) - 15(9)}$
- B $\dfrac{2000}{15(9) - (2x + 15)(2x + 9)}$
- C $\dfrac{2000}{(2x + 15)(2x + 9)}$
- D $\dfrac{2000}{15(9)x^2}$